BEHAVE!

HOW TO GET 100% OF YOUR WORKERS FULLY ENGAGED.

BILL BURNETT

WITH

RAJ JAYARAMAN, ANUP MANCHANDA,
HOWARD SCHWEDEL, GLENN TURNER

Special discounts on bulk quantities of this book are available (10 or more copies). Contact Books@thnk2grow.com

Published by THNK2GROW

ISBN: 1480120243
ISBN-13: 978-1480120242

Cover art by Arthur Allen Zdrinc

(847)970-2993

www.arthurzdrinc.com

TABLE OF CONTENTS

Preface

Close your eyes for half a minute and imagine your organization where everyone loves what they do and is doing exactly what needs to be done. How would it feel to know that the company is running well and you can now focus your energy on doing what you love to do? Moreover, all this is exists because you put in place a methodology that gets all your employees fully engaged. Take a moment and actually do it: close your eyes and imagine what it would feel like.

Feels good, right?!

This is a business book, and it's not really about feeling good. Feeling good is a nice fringe benefit. It's really about the money and the money is big.

Operating margin is extraordinarily sensitive to the amount of discretionary thinking being done by employees. What is shocking is how big the number is. Towers Watson published a study correlating operating margin to the portion of employees who are fully engaged. Where engagement is low, the operating margin is slightly less than 10%. Where engagement is high, the average margin is over 27%.

When employees are looking for issues, thinking about ways to solve problems, and actually implementing these changes, the average difference in the company's operating margin is a three fold greater margin than comparison companies. It is a huge difference (and it's just the average[1]).

Now, if you are like many CEOs you might be thinking to yourself, 'well this doesn't really apply to me because my margins are pretty healthy right where they are'. It is possible (although unlikely) that you're right. Here is a simple test. Think of seven of your lower level employees. Pick two top performers, two bottom performers, and three average performers. Now list all the changes each of them implemented in the past year to improve your operating margin. Six out of the seven should have changes next to their names and on average each of the seven should have between three and four such changes.

Do companies actually see this level of performance? Yes, and perhaps the easiest example is the NUMMI plant in California. While this took place a couple of decades ago, (the plant is now making the TESLA Model S) it is an example that has been well studied and documented. Many years before Tesla took over, the plant had been GM's worst plant with a 'terrible' unionized workforce who produced the most expensive, worst quality car.

---

[1] Interestingly where employee engagement is "high" on this chart, the proportion of highly engaged employees typically does not exceed 50%. CEOs repeatedly insist to us that if you could get 100% of your employees fully engaged the operating margin would be substantially better than what Towers Watson reports.

GM threw in the towel and closed the plant, laying off all the workers. A couple of years later Toyota, in a joint venture with GM, reopened the plant hiring back the same union workers.

Since Toyota had sent engineers to set up the plant in the first place, and since Toyota had lots of expertise in setting up assembly lines, you wouldn't expect there'd be very much room for improvement. But you'd be wrong, just as you'd be wrong to think there's no room for improvement in your own operating margin.

Unlike GM, Toyota structured the workplace to enable workers to give the company their discretionary thinking. It took six months before the hardened GM union workers actually believed that Toyota wanted their ideas. But once that happened, it opened a floodgate of ideas. More than 10,000 worker ideas were implemented in just the first year of operation. This pace kept up every year. For example, ten years into operations the thousands of ideas from 95% of workers in that tenth year alone saved the plant $27 million per year (Stanford University Graduate School of Business 2004).

How did NUMMI compare to similar plants in the USA. When compared to the plant most similar to it, in the first year of operation alone, the NUMMI plant was 57% more efficient. (Krafcik 1986) NUMMI produced the same number of cars as the comparison GM plant, but with much fewer defects and with half the people! Which plant would you want to own?

Often people assume that what made this work were Toyota's famous Quality Circles. However, that's not what drove this performance. In fact, Toyota did not implement those circles in NUMMI until the plant had been running for several years. (Adler, Goldoftas and Levine 1999) What Toyota did was find a way to get employees to give the workplace their discretionary thinking, then enabled the employees to implement changes.

People call this *'engagement'*.

So why don't more companies leverage this NUMMI experience? Actually, lots of companies have been trying to do just that for years. Unfortunately the 'experts' in the field are treating symptoms and not the underlying problem. Every year companies employ the same engagement strategies and get the same disappointing results. The strategies include:

- ✓ *Articulate and Share Our Intrinsically Good Vision*
- ✓ *Define Core Values – Hire, Fire, Promote*
- ✓ *Communicate Like Crazy.*
- ✓ *Reward & Recognize*
- ✓ *Set SMART Goals*
- ✓ *Foster Trust – Up, Down, Sideways in the Company*
- ✓ *Provide Career Direction and Training*
- ✓ *Sponsor Well-being Programs*

These all feel like the right things to be doing. And, we've been at this for years with results that are spectacularly disappointing. Companies like Gallup, Towers Watson, Blessing White, Right Management and many others have been reporting on levels of employee engagement over the last several years. What do their measurements show? That the level of highly engaged workers continues to hover between 25% and 40% of the workforce. What we're doing to address this opportunity isn't working. Of course that doesn't stop us from continuing to do the same things over and over again in the belief that 'this time we'll get it right!'

But these tactics miss the real issue. Fundamentally, it's not so much a question of how to engage workers. The right question is how do we stop disengaging workers.

If you are like most business leaders, you are putting up with disengaged employees. A recent study by human resources consulting firm Towers Watson showed that over 25% of employees around the world are disengaged. In the United States, each disengaged employee costs the employer an average of $22,000 annually in lost productivity.[2] That means, for every disengaged employee you fired, you'd be $22,000 better off, even if you replaced that employee with one who was merely somewhat engaged.

These somewhat engaged employees make up another 40-60% of the workforce. While these employees are not costing you money, their net contribution is very small when compared to that of fully engaged employees.

If you could somehow transform your disengaged, unengaged, and somewhat engaged workers to fully engaged workers, you'd be getting your full measure of discretionary thinking. According to a Gallup study, a fully engaged employee is worth 240% more than an employee with lesser engagement (Van Allen 2009)[3]. Fully engaged employees are the ones carrying the load.

Picture this: You are the captain of your small boat, steering the tiller. Ahead of the boat and swimming furiously are your fully engaged employees, pulling you along. Every few yards one of these employees dives to the sea floor, grabs a handful of valuable treasure, and tosses it into the boat.

Swimming alongside the boat are your somewhat engaged

---

[2] Based on a recent Gallup study reporting $350 billion in total lost productivity in the USA.

[3] The difference between the Gallup study at 240% and Towers Watson at 170% is that the Towers Watson study only looked at operating margin while Gallup included the impact of innovation on top line growth as well as margin growth.

employees. If they happen to swim into a little treasure they'll toss it towards the boat; some treasures may even land in the boat. But these employees are mostly just swimming alongside you.

Behind the boat, hanging onto ropes and being pulled along by the boat, are your disengaged employees. Some are even swimming in the wrong direction and off at angles, impeding progress and making it hard for you to keep the boat on course.

Keep in mind, you're paying each of these employees to be there, and you're paying each one about the same amount. If an employee isn't swimming hard at the front of the boat, then should you be paying for that employee at all?

The answer is clear: You should only be paying for fully engaged employees.

The purpose of this book is to help you convert those hanging off the back of the boat, or swimming in the wrong direction, or idly swimming alongside you, into highly motivated and fully engaged employees throwing treasure into your boat. The end result should be that you are leading and paying only for highly motivated, fully engaged employees.

We're going to show you how to get there without firing a whole bunch of people. Companies that have done this sort of thing have discovered that very few employees don't fit. Since most people would rather be fully engaged in their work than not, you may only have one or two employees who realize they are on the wrong crew and let go of the rope.

We've worked hard to make our methodology simple to implement. Otherwise, it wouldn't get done.

While the methodology is simple to execute, it takes hard work, some time, and leadership commitment. However, you start to see results almost immediately, and we measure that.

No book, not this one or any other, is going to *do* anything for you. The work required to implement is yours to do. As you begin the journey toward full engagement of your workers, you will be required to challenge your tightly held beliefs and your natural resistance to change. You will need to build trust with employees who are not fully engaged, who may be skeptical and will need time to realize that what you're doing is genuine. You will need to bring to the table a little courage to face this challenge. But if you're like every other CEO we have ever worked with, courage is something you already have.

Our Behavioral Advantage™ methodology described in this book is based on our years of real-world experience and a solid body of scientific work.[4] Every tool must pass three criteria: it must be simple to use; it must be proven to work over several years; and we can point to a scientific reason why it works[5], it's not just luck. We promises three outcomes:

- A stronger bottom line that will sustain longer.
- Physically healthier employees. The methodology brings stability, consistency, and clarity to everyone in the organization, which relieves negative stress for a positive impact on general health.
- A boost in employee happiness. The methodology enables workers to get *Identity* and *Meaning* from their work, which

---

[4] While much of this research applies globally, some of the psychological research was conducted principally in Western, Educated, Industrialized, Rich, Democratic (WEIRD) societies (Henrich, Heine and Norenzayan 2010). Thus, we cannot claim that the methods in the book apply to every company everywhere.

[5] Much of the science in this book is based on work done by behavioral economists. They perform experiments that give them a definitive answer for the scope of that experiment. Then they will look at the implications of the experiment and extrapolate the results into other areas. When we say 'scientific reason' it is often these extrapolations. It's not as good a science as physics, but better than no science at all. Besides, we already know the tools work.

positively impacts happiness and well-being including the CEO's. It is a very nice fringe benefit.

When we have the privilege to implement Behavioral Advantage™ with companies, we give them a simple guarantee and we'll place the bulk of our compensation on achieving this result:

100% of your employees will be fully engaged.

At this point, you know what you want to accomplish – to get the best possible operating margin and robust organic top-line growth. You get that when 100% of your employees give your enterprise their discretionary thinking. The question is how to do that. We know the traditional list of activities on page *iv* does not get us there. The question is, 'What does?" This book is a 'how-to' book which answers that question.

.

Acknowledgements

Several people kindly offered to help us by reading the book and pointing out errors, and we want to thank them for this. They are: Alan Arnett, Arun Balakrishnan, Tally Bonlender, Vishali Chandramouli, Cheryl Corman, Richard Damisch, Michael Edgar, Bob Gately, and Casey Karl.

Whenever you crowd-source the editing of a book, errors may still slip through. If you find an error, please send it via e-mail to errors@thnk2grow.com. With your permission, we will happily add your name to the Acknowledgements next time we revise the text.

As principal author, I also want to thank my business partners, Raj Jayaraman, Anup Manchanda, Howard B. Schwedel, and Glenn M. Turner, who help me flesh out the ideas and test some of the tool formats. They have been a joy to work with.

Bill Burnett
February 2013

//

Part 1

Introduction

"It has become almost a truism in American management that the human resource is of all economic resources the one least efficiently used, and that the greatest opportunity for improved economic performance lies in the improvement of the effectiveness of people..."

Peter F. Drucker 1954

Behavior is all you get from your employees. It is what you pay for. Their behavior determines what gets done, how well it gets done, how much money your company makes, how fast you grow, and what reputation you enjoy. Behavior is what your employees say and do. It is all you get from them and all you pay for.

The more you roll the dice on employee behavior, the more you roll the dice on your results. Rolling the dice on your people's behavior is both foolish and <u>unnecessary</u>. Very few companies do a great job of getting the right behaviors from all employees. It's been done, of course, and a great example is what happened at the NUMMI plant in Freemont, California.

1

Other companies understand the value of getting the right behaviors but don't know how to do it. What we will do here is give you a methodology to get those right behaviors and motivate them. When you have all your employees exhibiting the right behaviors with high levels of motivation, you have a fully engaged workforce. It is this kind of workforce that produces extraordinary results.

In 2012, the Boston Research Group, along with Research Data Technology and The Center for Effective Organizations at the University of Southern California, conducted a study that surveyed over 36,000 employees from the C-suite to the front line, across 18 countries (The How Report). One finding from the report jumps off the page: when employees had the opportunity to self-govern their behavior, the company out-performed other types of management structures on all 14 measures used in the study.

As the report states: "We truly have entered the era of behavior."

We do not challenge the outcomes reported, or that it was the self-governed group that produced those outcomes. In fact we agree enthusiastically on that. However, we do challenge what the report claims next. The report goes on to say, "The organization's purpose and values inform decision-making and guide all employee and company behavior. In short, people act on the basis of a set of core principles and values" (LRN Corporation 2011). This implies that in addition to employees self-governing their behaviors as the distinguishing feature, their behaviors are also governed by a set of core principles and values that align with the company's core values. (The problem is that correlation does not mean causation, and based on other research we will challenge the role that values play in governing behavior shortly.)

What makes the environment self-governing is the accountability structure. In self-governing environments, the accountability structure is *Peer-to-Peer Accountability,* where every employee is responsible for helping every other employee manage his or her behavior to drive great results.

Every company seeks to manage employee behavior. It usually falls to the boss to do this. For most managers, it is a reactive process. The manager responds to a behavior that is great or to one that is bad. Otherwise, the manager is silent on behavior. It's surprising that we focus on proactive management in other areas of the business and assume that we can be reactive when it comes to behavior. Establishing core values feels proactive; however, the mistake companies make is in believing that the values will govern employee behavior.

The idea expressed in the How Report's summary, and shared in many other places, is that if we establish our values, then the right behaviors will follow. It is a common belief in the marketplace that you need to define your core values because they define your culture and your employees' behavior. Then, if you use these values to hire people who share these values you will get the culture you're after. Culture is only evidenced by the behaviors of your employees. Recently, a European CEO told me he doesn't believe in corporate culture. He says lots of business managers think culture is something different from behavior. All you get is behavior and talking about culture is a red herring. "Focus on behavior!" he says.

We think he is right. It adds nothing to talk about company culture. As humans, we seek to understand the world around us. We dig to try to discover as much as we can and build models to help describe what we observe. This builds complexity. We look for nuances and then exploit nuances and in the process make the topic more understandable. A by-product of this is that the whole structure becomes more complex. We love to create classifications and then layer classifications on top of classifications. Usually this helps us understand something more precisely. Although, not always.

The idea of 'culture' is a classification. It is there to allow us to talk about behavior in some broad and general way. However, because it is hard to define in a tangible way, it adds an unnecessary layer of complexity.

Our human ability to solve problems usually involves simplification. This is often why people who are not the traditional experts in an industry are the ones creating innovative approaches. Outsiders often see right through complexity and can define a problem with a new perspective. We are going to abandon any further discussion of culture. Behavior is all you get and all we need to talk about.

We are going to start our conversation by challenging a commonly held belief. You likely hold this belief. It turns out that it is human nature that once we hold a belief for a substantial length of time, the belief becomes immune to evidence to the contrary. This happens remarkably often to all of us, including scientists, academicians and even intelligence analysts. We want to caution you that this may be your reaction as well, despite the quality of the evidence to the contrary and the remarkable lack of supporting evidence for the currently held belief.

One famous example of this steadfast dedication to a belief was the response to the Michaelson-Morely experiment, which measured the speed of light. Physicists Michaelson and Morely did something very simple. The laws of Newtonian Physics say that if you are standing still and throw a ball with a certain force X, it will leave your hand at fifty kilometers per hour. Likewise, if you are standing on a train going sixty kilometers per hour, and you throw the ball in the direction of travel with the same force X, it will leave your hand at one hundred ten kilometers per hour (fifty + sixty). In 1887, E.W. Morley and A.A. Michelson decided to do a measurement that depended upon the difference between the velocity of light as it is beamed with the speed of the rotation of the earth pushing it (in Rome, Chicago, and New York that's about 783 miles per hour[6]) and the speed of light perpendicular to the earth's rotation. The idea was that the light beam that has the speed of the earth's rotation behind it must be going faster than the light beam that does not have that incremental speed behind it.

To their surprise, no difference was detected. The scientific community knew that something was wrong with the way Morley and Michelson did their experiment because you cannot violate the laws of physics. It perplexed scientists for years because they couldn't find the error. The findings were inconsistent with Newton's laws of motion. Although the experiment was rebuilt and repeated several times with the same result, the physics community chose the theory over the evidence. They chose to believe that either the experiment was somehow faulty, or that there was a yet undiscovered other force influencing the result.

Then, in 1905, along came Albert Einstein who showed them a different theory to explain the actual results. Did the physics community jump for joy, shouting, "Eureka, we have a solution!"?

Of course not, nobody jumped for joy at Einstein's solution. The poor guy's findings languished in the patent office for several years after he published his now famous papers. Newton's hold on the minds of physicists was very strong. Einstein might have been ignored completely had it not been for

---

[6] As calculated http://www.thevlecks.net/rmj/earth.html Accessed on 10/31/2012. At the Equator the Earth's rotation is about 1038 miles per hour.

Max Planck, and Einstein didn't fully convince Planck until 1911.

A more recent example occurred when, in a meeting of economists, one of their members, Maurice Allais, devised a choice experiment that they all participated in. What they did not realize was that the choices they made in the experiment proved that a theory they all loved was wrong. Allais was excited to reveal this bombshell at the end of the meeting, and anticipated that the economists would be immediately convinced to give up the theory and adopt one that better described the real outcome. Even this most powerful and personal demonstration of the data failed to unseat the theory. The economists (including several who would later win Nobel Prizes) stubbornly continued to use the faulty theory as part of their economics tool kits despite its now famous flaw.

The point is, here we have a bunch of scientists whose life work is the search for truth, finding themselves hamstrung by a quirk of human psychology called *Theory Induced Blindness*, a term coined by Daniel Kahneman (Kahneman 2011, 277). It is what Einstein recognized as well when he said, "*It is the theory that decides what can be observed*" (Salam 1990, 99).

Chances are that you are not a physicist or an economist. You may have even more difficulty seeing the flaw in a belief you hold dear. All we can ask you to do is to listen to the evidence and sleep on it. We will only be presenting a small portion of the research that's available. However, it represents over seven decades of similar studies. These studies provide very strong evidence that consistently shows that the commonly held belief is wrong.

Here is the commonly held belief:

Our values drive our behavior.

This notion about values and behavior is not unreasonable. The problem is that over time, it has hardened into a presumption. We have said this so often that we've come to accept it as true without even thinking to look for supporting evidence. We accept it presumptively. Thus, when someone asserts that values guide behavior, we are far less likely to ask them to prove it. However, when someone asserts that values don't drive behavior, we are likely to say, "Prove it!"

The idea that values regulate behavior is an appealing idea, and we'd love for it to be true. We love the idea of our behavior being guided by an inner true compass. Unfortunately, it is not true.

This notion is a popular idea with business book authors. For example, Patrick Lencioni's 2012 book *The Advantage* suggests that the answer to the question of 'how employees behave' is embodied in the company's core values. Lencioni states that these values provide the guidance for the behavior of workers at all levels in the company.

Most business people take this idea for granted. If you will recall, the study mentioned at the beginning of this introduction simply inserted this idea into its conclusion that values caused the self-governing employees to produce the right behaviors. The thinking suggests that if you hire people who share your core values, then they will behave accordingly. It has been said so often that it is generally accepted as true without question. However, if values do not regulate behavior, then hiring people on that basis may be less important. It would also mean you could not rely on values to guide behavior, which would open the door to a big disconnect between values and behaviors.

The question is this: "Do values actually guide human behavior, or does something else drive behavior?" If the answer is that values do not determine human behavior, then something else must. And since behavior is all we get, we'd better find out what that something else is, and put it to work to get the behaviors we want and get our money's worth.

As CEO of your company, you are paying for nothing more than behavior. You pay for great behavior, where your employee is highly motivated and doing the right things in the right ways. You pay for mediocre behavior, where your employee is doing the job, and is not particularly motivated to go the extra mile. You pay for unproductive behavior, where your employee is doing something other than being productive. And you also pay for destructive behavior, where your employee is misbehaving with a customer, or interfering with or undermining a colleague.

You should only be paying for great behavior.

Behavior Matters.

Human behavior in a company is the single most significant determinant of the success or failure of that company. Influencing that behavior with expertise demands a critical understanding of what works, and what doesn't. The idea that values play a determining role in behavior is about governing behavior. When we talk about values driving behavior, the goal is behavior. Behavior is what matters.

The roots of the idea that values are precepts that inform our personal, professional, and political behavior come from philosophers and psychologists. In 1973, social psychologist Milton Rokeach said, "Values are determinants of virtually all kinds of behavior that could be called social behavior or social action…" (Rokeach 1973, 24). This theme is behind the Core Values concepts in Collins and Porras' now famous book, *Built to Last*. Their idea was that if you hire people who share the company's core values, their behavior will be consistent with what the company is looking for (Collins and Porras 1996). Values like communication, respect, integrity, and excellence should produce behaviors consistent with those company values.

The concept is echoed in how we often talk about people. It is the notion that a person *is guided by his or her own internal compass*.

A recent study in the UK suggests that if this popular idea is true, then we have reason to be concerned about the future. One value that often stands as the barometer of all important values is *integrity*.

> *It turned out that the integrity level for youth was significantly below the integrity level for people middle-aged and older. As the study summary pointed out, it is possible that people get more integrity as they age. But there is also evidence to suggest that it is likely that people learn their values when young, and stick with them throughout their lives. This latter view would be more worrisome and the author of the study suggests, "...there are reasons to be pessimistic about this since research on political values suggests that people tend to acquire their basic political beliefs in adolescence and these do not change very much as they grow older." If this is also true of integrity, then the future looks darker.* (Whiteley 2012)

Perhaps it's not that dark, particularly if it turns out that values do not govern behavior.

Values and Behavior

On May 11, 1960, Nazi SS Colonel Adolph Eichmann was captured in Argentina and shortly thereafter whisked off to Israel to be tried for war crimes. He was responsible for the deportation and ultimate deaths of 5 million people. At his trial, he testified that "I never did anything, great or small, without obtaining in advance express instructions from Adolf Hitler or any of my superiors." His defense was that he was following orders.

This was the same defense used by many of Eichmann's fellow Nazis during trials at Nuremberg. This claim by Eichmann inspired Yale University psychologist Stanley Milgram. He wondered if there was any legitimacy to the claim. He decided to conduct experiments to test the assertion. He set out to measure the willingness of study participants to obey an authority figure who has instructed them to perform acts that conflicted with their personal conscience (their values). You may be familiar with this famous Milgram experiment.

In July 1961, three months into the Eichmann trial, Milgram posted a public announcement inviting participants to a study of memory. He paid each volunteer subject $4.50 ($34 in 2012 dollars) for an hour of their time. They were paid for showing up, and were not otherwise coerced into participating in the experiment. The volunteer was told that he (the subjects were all male in the first experiment) was participating in a "learning experiment" ostensibly set up to study the effects of punishment on memory. The volunteer subject came into the room and he and another person who appeared to be a volunteer drew slips of paper from a hat. All the slips had "Teacher" written on them. The second volunteer was actually a confederate in the experiment. The confederate looked at the slip he'd drawn and said, "My slip says learner." The volunteer's slip said "Teacher."

They then went into a room and the confederate "Learner" was strapped into a chair and electrodes were attached to his arms. The subject "Teacher" was then taken into an adjoining room where the "Learner" could be heard, but not seen.

Then, as part of the set-up, the subject "Teacher" was first given a 45 volt shock from the electro-shock generator (an official looking piece of equipment). This was a sample shock to let the "Teacher" know that it was quite painful. The "Teacher" then read a list of 30 word pairs to the "Learner", who was instructed to memorize the list. When the shocking apparatus was all set, the "Teacher" would read one word from the word pair list and then four possible answers. If the answer given by the "Learner" was correct, the "Teacher" went on to the next word. If the answer was wrong, the "Teacher" pressed the button to administer a shock to the "Learner." After each shock, the voltage dial was advanced by 15 volts. The device showed 30 levels from 15 volts to 450 volts.

Dr. Milgram placed a person wearing a lab coat and holding a clipboard next to the "Teacher." Whenever the "Teacher" protested or hesitated to administer an electric shock, the technician would insist that the subject continue with the experiment. On the other side of the wall, a press of the shock button triggered a tape recorder, which played the painful reaction from the "Learner" to the electric shocks. As the voltage increased, the screaming and begging became more urgent. The confederate on that side of the wall would bang on the wall in protest. Of course, the shocks were not real and the confederate was only acting.

Milgram found: "No subject stopped prior to administering Shock Level 20. (At this lethal level — 300 volts — the victim kicked on the wall and no longer provided answers to the teacher's multiple-choice questions.) Of the 40 subjects, 5 refused to obey the experimental commands beyond the 300-volt level. Four more subjects administered one further shock, and then refused to go on. Two broke off at the 330-volt level, and one each at 345, 360, and 375 volts." (Milgram 1963) All the rest, 26 "Teachers" in all, gave the full 450 volts to the "Learner."

Milgram concluded, "Ordinary people, simply doing their jobs, and without any particular hostility on their part, can become agents in a terrible, destructive process. Moreover, even when the destructive effects of their work become patently clear, and they are asked to carry out actions incompatible with fundamental standards of morality, relatively few people have the resources needed to resist authority." (Milgram, Obedience to Authority 1974)

Milgram's experiment isn't the only example of this surprising behavior. This notion of people acting in ways that conflict with their values pops up all over the place. I mentioned the Milgram experiment on LinkedIn and got the following story from Bob Gately:

"A Ph.D. grad school professor was from Moscow and we used to talk about the USSR and how and why the party did such terrible things to its own citizens. I said, "In the US that would never happen." He replied, "Just because you wouldn't do it does not mean everyone else wouldn't do it." I then remembered a barrack' conversation in Saigon nine months after the Tet Offensive in 1968. Several of our barracks mates had lived through the Tet Offensive and shared their experiences. One airman asked, "Would you shoot an enemy soldier who was bound and gagged if an officer ordered you to do it?" I was stunned by how many airmen said yes, since we all went through the same basic training and were taught that doing so could land us in jail."

The Milgram experiment has since been repeated in different settings and in different cultures. The results of these ongoing reruns consistently support the finding that ordinary people do behave in ways that are inconsistent with their values.[7] It is the context, the environment, that matters.

More recently, Dan Ariely has been doing some very entertaining and enlightening work around cheating. Most people do not think of themselves as cheaters. However, in his cleverly designed experiments, Ariely demonstrates that we all cheat. We don't cheat by very much, but we do cheat.

I was recently at a networking meeting and talked about Ariely's findings. One of the people listening protested, insisting he did not cheat! I then asked him how he got to the meeting. "I drove," he replied. "I take it then," I asked, "that you obeyed the speed limit the whole way here?" He paused for several seconds. "Well, I don't want to self-incriminate. So let me just say this: I see your point." This is a simple example of the influence of social context on our values.

In the USA it is fair to say, "We all speed." And we all feel quite comfortable with this unlawful activity. We don't think of ourselves as habitual criminals, even though speeding is a violation of the law. Of course, the telltale sign that we know we are doing something wrong is our inclination to slow down whenever we spot a police car.

The degree to which we speed when driving will be influenced by others around us. Often you might be driving along at a reasonable 20% above the speed limit, when suddenly you'll be passed by a pulse of cars, four or five of them, all going much faster than your comfortable 20% margin. It isn't one car, it is a small group of them. Some brave speeder started it and others

---

[7] Eichmann's 'I was only following orders' defense did not persuade his Israeli judges. For his part in the Nazi enterprise, Eichmann was found guilty in Jerusalem and in May 1962 became the only person who's been executed in Israel on conviction by a civilian court.

joined in. If there's a police car ahead, these four or five cars will quickly disappear into the normal flow, which also has abandoned the normal 20% margin for one closer to 5% in response to the presence of the "Law."

This idea of following the herd can create an insidious problem. A large bank in New York provided its CEO with a helicopter and a limousine, both available 24 hours, 7 days a week, as a perk of the job. The company president didn't enjoy a helicopter, but he did have the use of a full-time limousine and drivers. Executive vice presidents didn't have either, but in a pinch they could call a car service. Actually, the car service was available to all employees for work-related purposes.

The example of this would be a female employee of the bank working late into the evening in a building that wasn't in the safest neighborhood. She was supposed to call the car service for a ride home in those circumstances. The 60 hours-per-week work ethic in the bank meant that many people worked late and took limos home every night. They simply called the service, got picked up, and upon reaching their destination signed a slip of paper.

In time, some of the more senior executives began to use the car service slightly differently. If they had a visitor in town, they might use the car service to go from home to dinner with their guest and back. They would justify the use of the service by saying that the dinner conversation was somehow related to business. All the slips of paper they signed were put through the financial process whereby junior analysts were privy to the behavior.

No junior analyst was going to object to this use by executives for fear of reprisals. Nevertheless, word got around. A little while later, other employees began to use the service similarly, following the lead of their superiors. Eventually, it became quite common for any Manhattan-based employee to go out on the town on a weekend, drink a bit too much, and call the car service for a ride home. The justification? "Surely it is in the company's best interests to see to it that I get safely home." Eventually, no justification was needed; it was part of the routine.

After a while, the service became quite expensive for the company. One day, when looking at expenses, the CEO noticed this line item. He asked a few questions, then summarily banned all uses of the car service as punishment. This meant that if you worked in a bad part of town, then you would be taking a risk if you stayed late. Immediately the Manhattan workweek dropped to nearer 40 hours per week.

This change did not become immediately apparent to the CEO. When it did, he reinstated the car service with careful monitoring of use. However, the workweek never fully returned to the previous level. It seemed that the social norm around the length of the workweek had been altered, too.

The behavior of those around us does influence our own behavior. Leaders can have a particularly strong influence. In his 2012 book, *The (Honest) Truth About Dishonesty,* Dan Ariely included a letter from Jonah, a disappointed employee of an economic consulting firm. (Ariely, The (Honest) Truth 2012, 34)

The consulting company supplied research services to a law firm. The law firm would add this work to the client's bill with a mark-up. Within the consulting firm, the incentive program encouraged overstating hours worked on a project. Moreover, the analysts worried about their jobs if they billed less than their peers. Everyone, from the most senior employee to the most junior analyst, overstated his or her hours. "One person bills every hour he is monitoring his email for a project, whether or not he receives any work to do. He is 'on-call,' he says" (Ariely, The (Honest) Truth 2012, 35-36). The exception was one ethical employee who insisted he only bill actual hours and consequently billed at a rate 20% below the norm. When it became necessary to reduce the size of the firm, the first to go was the only honest employee, sending a clear, if unintended, message to all employees -- Cheat!

What would you expect your employees would do if thrust into a similar situation?

Even in vehicle emission testing we find widespread cheating. In some states, vehicle emission testing is done by a state run facility. In other states, this testing is done by private entities under license from the state. There are some incentives to cheat where private entities are involved. Where the testing facility can offer to fix the car to enable it to pass the inspection, there is an incentive to fail a car initially, fix it, and then charge for both the test and the repair. Another incentive encourages the tester to pass a vehicle to ensure that the driver will bring the car to the same test site the next year. As a consequence, cheating happens.

In a study of such cheating at vehicle emission testing facilities, it became clear that the degree of cheating depended on the organization. In some organizations there was more cheating than in others. A tester could lose his or her job if caught cheating. However, if that is how the facility operated, the tester would join in and cheat. The study suggested that with much repetition of the cheating, the bad behavior becomes ethically normal. "The results from our models strongly suggest that individual ethical behavior is influenced by the ethics of the employer." (Pierce and Snyder 2008)

Social Context and Behavior

The most interesting point about the idea that values regulate behavior is that it is wrong. Values do not drive behavior. Social context trumps values. It is the influence of the social environment that causes us to do things every day that conflict with our values. The four values we mentioned earlier - communication, respect, integrity, and excellence - were Enron's values, and we know something about the behavior of some Enron employees.

If you read business literature you will occasionally come across descriptions of people being guided by their "internal compass." As we saw in the Milgram experiment, some people were ultimately influenced by their internal compass. These people eventually stopped shocking  the "Learner" despite the urgings of the authority figure standing over them. None of the forty had an internal compass strong enough to steer them entirely clear of the values violation. Everyone in the experiment pressed the shock button at least 13 times. We believe we are guided by our values, but as humans, that guide is less powerful than we'd like to imagine. This is true of you, and of me, and of everyone we work with. The power of the herd, and of individuals in a power role, can be overwhelming to what Abraham (?) Lincoln called "the better angels of our nature."

The easy leap we make in believing that values guide behavior comes from motivational theory. In motivational theory, we use the words "needs" and "values" almost interchangeably to describe the cause of an instance of behavior. We say that basic human behaviors, like eating, are motivated by needs. We say that other behaviors, such as generosity, are driven by values.

For example, I found a wallet containing six $100 bills and the owner's driver's license and business card. What motivates me to contact the owner and return the money is believed to be a 'value.' In this case the 'value' is assumed to be honesty. We then make a theoretical leap that generalizes that 'value' as having the power to almost always produce that behavior.

We make a presumptive leap when we say that the act of returning the wallet was caused by the value of honesty. As I was the person who returned the wallet, I know that it wasn't honesty or altruism that drove me to do it. Rather it was an excellent opportunity to create the persona I wanted to be in the eyes of my children. I wanted them to see me as the honest person I like to think I am. (Thanks to Milgram and Ariely I now know I'm fallible too.)

Lincoln made a great point about assuming that values like altruism drive behavior:[8]

> "*Riding horseback on the campaign trail in his recently purchased clean suit, Lincoln passed a pig stuck in the mud on a river bank. Lincoln looked at the squealing pig, and then at his new clothes, and decided to ride on. After a mile or so, he turned his horse around, went back and proceeded to free the pig, which would have otherwise certainly drowned. The effort cost him the cleanliness of his suit. He scraped off as much of the mud as he could and rode on to the inn where he was to spend the night. When the innkeeper remarked on his filthy clothing Lincoln said, "Oh, I have a very good reason for my*

---

[8] Apparently there are several versions of this story. This is how I heard it as a young man in a marvelous philosophy class as told by the late professor Dean Kolitch making a point about altruism.

muddy clothes. You see down the road a ways a hog was stuck in the mud at the riverbank and would have drowned had I not gone to its aid." The innkeeper started to remark about being a Good Samaritan, but Lincoln stopped him, "Oh the sow benefitted; however, I must admit, the good reason was a selfish one. I am campaigning for office and have a debate with my opponent in the morning. Had I not rescued the pig, thoughts of its peril and squeals would have kept me awake all night. If I am to win tomorrow's debate I must sleep, and now I will."

We often assume that a particular value drives behavior when it may be something else entirely.

In the second volume of this book, we will address many factors that influence decision-making. These decisions then drive subsequent behavior. These influencing factors usually have nothing to do with values. In fact, most of these influencers are on a subconscious level. Thus, on top of the influence of the herd on our behavior, is the background stuff that goes on in our own heads. The notion business "experts" have about values driving behavior is wrong.

While we cannot count on our values to govern behavior on a sustained basis, the good news is that we can still use the power of values to influence a specific instances of behavior. Values do influence behavior in a powerful way, but they only work when they are front-and-center. You cannot publish your values and expect that they will drive behavior. Here are a couple of examples of how values influence behavior in this transitory way.

For example, in Dan Ariely's experiments where people are afforded the opportunity to cheat, they tend to cheat a little bit, just as we do when we drive faster than the speed limit. Interestingly, he has found that he can eliminate the cheating altogether by preceding the task with a values reminder.

In a cheating experiment using groups of MIT students, he reminded some of the groups that the task was governed under the MIT Honor Code. In those groups, nobody cheated. (*Ariely humorously points out that this occurred even though MIT doesn't actually have an honor code.*) (Ariely, Predictably Irrational 2008, 289).

In another one of Ariely's fascinating studies on cheating the only variable he changed was this. One group was asked to recall 10 books that they'd read in high school. The other group was asked to write down the Ten Commandments. Then both groups were given the same opportunity to cheat. Their aggregated scores were compared to the aggregated scores of a control group, which had no opportunity to cheat. When the scores were compared, the group that had to recall the 10 books had scores about a third higher that the people who couldn't cheat. This group cheated. But the people who were tasked to recall the Ten Commandments didn't cheat at all. How do we know that? Because their aggregate scores were nearly identical to the aggregate scores of the people who could not cheat.

The change in context does not have to involve a value like honesty or an honor code. It can be a more subtle value around the value we place in being good to one another.

In a study reported to the Radiological Society of North America in December 2008 Dr. Yehonatan N. Turner reported that more incidental findings were discovered by radiologists when the patient's image accompanied the radiological image. Apparently, including the patient's photograph caused the radiologists to provide a more meticulous reading of the medical image. Three months later the same radiologists were shown previous examination images (that contained incidental findings) without the patient photo attached. In these cases the radiologists failed to report 80% of the incidental findings that had been reported in the original group.

We can also use other kinds of subtle reminders to cause people to modify their behavior for a short period of time.

We can get people to slow down to the suggested speed limit with a simple trick. In Chicago, as you approach the treacherous curve on Lake Shore Drive immediately south of Oak Street Beach, you are presented with a series of horizontal lines painted in the roadway. Their spacing changes as you pass over them to make you feel as though you are speeding up. As a result, you slow down before you reach the dangerous curve.[9]

Baby and Bath-Water

Does all this mean we should discard all the work we've done around articulating company values? No. All it means is that we can't rely on values to guide behavior. Core values serve a different purpose. Core values are created in conjunction with core purpose and become a part of the motivational superstructure for the business. We will talk about that shortly. But first, we will focus on getting the right behaviors.

If you're the owner of a company, you're paying for every instance of behavior that you get from your employees. You pay for hard working behaviors, for goofing off behaviors, and for behaviors that are destructive to your business.

In the next chapters, you will learn a method for dealing with behaviors such that you get the behaviors you want and eliminate the ones you don't. This means that you will end up paying for only the behaviors that move the business forward.

---

[9] You can see these horizontal lines by searching maps on the Internet for the Drake Hotel. Go due east of the hotel until you see Lake Shore Drive, switch to satellite view, and you will see the lines in the roadway.

You will only pay for behaviors that contribute to a healthy profit.

The right behaviors are not enough. You want to motivate those behaviors. Fully engaged employees deliver the right behaviors, fully motivated. When we work with a company to implement the tools under the Behavioral Advantage™ methodology, we guarantee 100% full engagement and stake most of our fee on that success.

Behavior

Employees behave in accordance with the guidance of the social context. In the study mentioned in the last chapter around the dishonesty of vehicle emissions testers the authors discovered something else in the data. Because testers are licensed, they are assigned a state license number that they use to identify themselves on testing documents. The same state license number persists across employers. This enabled the researchers to track them in different employment settings. *"When individuals work across different facilities, their behavior conforms to that of the facility that employs them. Our results suggest inspector behavior converges toward the norms of the employer nearly immediately, with little lag or gradual adaptation."* (Pierce and Snyder 2008, 4) Thus, the propensity of the tester to cheat depends on the social context. How much cheating everyone else is doing influences the individual tester's behavior. It is similar to speeding in a car. If you pull onto a road where all other cars are driving at the speed limit, so will you. If you go much faster than the traffic norm, then you'll likely feel pretty uncomfortable as the outlier.

In a hierarchical environment, the boss plays a important role in setting the social context. This is the notion that the boss is a role model. In an earlier example I introduced an economics consulting firm that expected its analyst to overestimate their billable hours on any project. Junior analysts behaved as their more superior colleagues behaved. However, because you are part of management, you might be tempted to argue that the management may not have been aware of this cheating. Perhaps management actually wanted analysts to bill actual hours, thus, it was the analysts fault for overestimate billable hours.

This raises a key tenet of the Behavioral Advantage™ : Leadership is responsible for the behavior of employees. This includes both defining the behaviors, and making sure they are followed correctly. If an employee does not exhibit the desired behavior then corrective action is called for. If an employee consistently fails to exhibit the desired behavior then leadership should afford the employee an opportunity to find more compatible work. Leadership owns behavior. (While leadership ultimately owns the responsibility, as you will see, the heavy lifting will be done by the peer group.)

This idea of leadership owning behavior is an empowering idea. It places accountability squarely where it has the most potential. Leadership takes ownership of behavior. This means that leadership is responsible for determining what behaviors will get the desired results. Leadership is also responsible for establishing an environment where individual employees have the opportunity to find ample self-motivation. (We will discuss motivation in detail in the next chapter.)

Only individual employees can exhibit the prescribed behavior. For that, they are accountable. You will boost the power of that accountability by introducing the concept of *Peer-to-Peer Accountability*. That is, the employee is not only accountable to the boss for delivering the right behaviors, but is also, and more immediately accountable to all peers in the company. In other words, you don't act one way when the boss is around, and then act in a different way when the boss is absent.

While we place the responsibility for defining behaviors squarely on the shoulders of leadership, when we get to motivation we broaden the responsibility to include the employee, the peer group, and lastly the leadership.

Peers have powerful influence. In fact, when we get to the topic of accountability we will focus on peer influence. This influence can be extraordinary, even in instances where almost nothing is obviously at stake for the influenced individual. For a little fun, look at the power of peer influence in the video showing how an individual conforms to the odd behavior of a group in an elevator:

http://www.youtube.com/watch?v=N7jUJUa77kk&feature=player_embedded%23!

The trick is to make this human inclination to conform to peer pressure work for us.

The importance of *Peer-to-Peer Accountability* is paramount. In the Boston Research Group study of the 36,000 employees (mentioned in the beginning of the introduction), *Peer-to-Peer Accountability* was a distinguishing characteristic in the most successful companies. This is what we intend to make explicit in the Behavioral Advantage™ method. *Peer-to-Peer Accountability* is, according to Pat Lencioni, is the most powerful and effective kind of accountability. *Peer-to-Peer Accountability* is the foundation of the accountability component of our Behavioral Advantage™ model.

In 1935 and 1937 Muzafer Sherif demonstrated the remarkable influence of peers. In his experiments he had subjects go into a pitch black room. This gave the subjects no frame of reference to detect movement. He then projected onto the wall a small spot of light instructing the subject to press a button when the light began to move. Once the subject pressed the button the light would remain lighted for two seconds. The subject was then asked to describe how much the spot of light moved. With no physical basis for detecting actual motion, the subject could not know that the light did not actually move. The subject's brain imagined the movement. This procedure was repeated many times with each subject. With each instance of the light being projected the subject would verbally report how far the light moved. The experimenter would record the reported distance.

What Sherif's study showed was that people will create a range of perceived movement, and once they've embraced that range, they will stay within the range, reporting the mode as near the midpoint. (Sherif, Factors in perception 1935) It was usually a narrow range. However, across the population of subjects, the individual ranges and modes could vary greatly. Some people would report the light moving two inches on average, for others the average would be closer to nine inches.

Then, Sherif wanted to find out if the range could be influenced by a second or third person in the room. He showed that while initial individual judgments in the group could be significantly different in the beginning, they converged within a narrowing band with each repetition of the experiment to the point where the individuals in their group reported almost exactly the same distances. Different groups locked in on quite different norms for their reported distances. Clearly the social environment influenced the reported perceived distances.

Later still, in 1937, he had a confederate deliberately report a narrow band with the subject in the room. (Sherif, Attitudes 1937) Irrespective of what the narrow band was (he varied the confederate's band), within a few iterations of displaying the light, the subject adopted the confederate's norm. The conclusion was obvious. We will adopt a norm even one that differs significantly from what we observed. There are many other similar studies that show we are beings who are easily influenced by the herd. The point is, behaviors are malleable while we believe that values are far more rigid.

However, there is more to behavior than that. I give you permission to photocopy the exercise below. Give it to one or two of your friends. In fact, do it yourself before you read further.

> Terry is thirty-one years old, single, outspoken, and intelligent. Terry's undergraduate degree was in philosophy at an ivy-league school and went on to pursue a law degree but got disgusted and quit. In college Terry was deeply concerned with social injustice and actively participated in civil rights and every other anti-discrimination movement. Please rank the following statements in order of probability of being true. 1= most true, 8= least true.

Row	Scenario	Rank
1	Terry is an elementary school teacher.	
2	Terry is an astronaut.	
3	Terry is an assistant manager in a rare books store.	
4	Terry is active in the gay rights movement.	
5	Terry is a member of the Democratic Party	
6	Terry is a bank assistant-manager	
7	Terry is an insurance salesperson	
8	Terry is a bank assistant-manager and is active in liberal political causes.	

Look at how you answered in line 6 and line 8. Most people will say line 6 (Terry is a bank assistant-manager)is a lower probability than line 8 (Terry is a bank assistant-manager and is active in liberal political causes.) This is because the story we build in our heads of Terry being both a bank assistant-manager and a person who is active in political movements is more coherent than the story that Terry is an assistant manager in a bank.[10] Of course in the field of probabilities the inclusive set cannot be less probable than one of its subsets. If Terry is a bank assistant-manager and a person who is active in political movements then it is at least equally probably that Terry is a bank assistant manager. If we believe that there are some bank assistant managers who are not active in political movements, then the probability that Terry is a bank assistant-manager and a person who is active in political movements must be less than the probability that Terry is simply a bank assistant-manager (as the Venn diagram indicates). As one CEO I worked with said, "*In our brains we tend to think that it is a more necessary condition that Terry is active in political movements than that Terry is a bank assistant manager. This causes us to screw up the probabilities. We answer a different question: Is it more likely that Terry is not active in political movements and happens to be a bank assistant manager; or that Terry is active in political movements and happens to be a bank assistant manager?*"

---

[10] The example is similar to, and inspired by, one developed by Daniel Kahneman.

We build stories in our heads. The coherence of these stories determines how we evaluate possibilities. Coherence is responsible for how we will perceive the probability of the outcome being true. We will come back to this behavior when we talk about decision-making in Volume Two[11]. We will present tools to enable you to overcome the many quirks in human behavior that influence and undermine good decision-making.

Behavioral Model

To get the behaviors we want and the results these behaviors will deliver, we will need to be good at all six components of the

Behavioral Model. Behavior, Motivation, and Accountability make up the core components of the model. Where these three

---

[11] Volume Two is due to be published in late 2013

components are working well, the business will enjoy the payoff of a fully engaged workforce. Leadership, Context, and Structure are the supporting components that ensure we can sustain Behavior, Motivation, and Accountability over time.

Behavior consists of the behaviors of our internal people. This includes both desired behaviors, and banned behaviors, at both the employee level and the leadership level. (We will focus on the leadership behaviors in chapter three.)

Motivation puts the energy behind the desired behaviors. The Behavioral Advantage™ methodology allows your employees to create *Identity* and *Meaning* through their work. We will cover this component in the next chapter.

Accountability means being liable or answerable. What makes accountability work in a business is more than being liable and answerable. It is the audit function that makes accountability a powerful concept. It is the discipline around making sure the answering actually takes place. (Rodgers and Hunter 1991) "What gets measured gets done." This is verification, and it must be timely. Discipline is what makes for effective accountability. The Behavioral Advantage™ methodology will install an active mechanism to ensure *Peer-to-Peer Accountability* is a disciplined routine.

Leadership covers the aspects of leadership behavior that engenders the needed employee behaviors. Leadership behaviors tend to be more complex because they influence motivation and motivation is sensitive to nuance. You will discover when you implement Behavioral Advantage™ that deciding what behavior is the right behavior requires a good deal of thought.

Context ensures that the needed behaviors, particularly for leadership behavior, are consistent with and supportive of the motivational component. Activity around Context simply ensures that you don't do something in Leadership that gets you the desired employee behavior but undermines the effectiveness of your motivational components.

Structure enables all members of the business the ability to address behaviors that push outside of what's allowed. Structure also allows your people to resolve unanticipated disputes before they become personal. Structure is a set of uniform policies that the CEO requires everyone to adhere to rigorously, beginning with himself or herself.

Step #1: Defining Behaviors

Defining behaviors is not a topic most managers are familiar with even though behavior is what they manage on a daily basis. Most behavior management is ad hoc. At any moment, the employee is either delivering the right behavior or not. The manager takes action to adjust the employee's behavior, perhaps in the moment or sometime later.

Most managers do not define and prescribe subordinate behavior. Rather, they react to good and bad behaviors when they see them. Unfortunately, we have learned in the past few years that much of this management is actually bad leadership and bad psychology. (R. I. Sutton 2010) Often the correction is unnecessary or self-defeating. This is sloppy management and delivers inconsistent behaviors. The Behavioral Advantage™ methodology will cause your managers to be more purposeful from now on. The first step is to define the behaviors you want from your employees.

You seek to define a set of behaviors that deliver the results you want. Humans are not robots. Any definition of behavior has to be around human behavior. We are trying to set the boundaries rather than get very granular. The behaviors we define must leave room for human interaction that is fun. "Laughter is encouraged" is a statement every company would be wise to include in its behavioral grid.

What is a Behavioral Grid?

A Behavioral Grid is a simple tool we use to help us define behaviors. It consists of a set of three columns labeled Key Company Attributes, Supporting Behaviors, and Banned Behaviors. This is a working document. You will likely refine it over time.

We start with an exercise that defines behaviors broadly across the company. However, the power of Behavioral Advantage™ is at the individual level. Your peer teams will follow a similar model to define the desired and banned behaviors for every position in the company.

KEY COMPANY ATTRIBUTES	SUPPORTING BEHAVIORS	BANNED BEHAVIORS

When we work with a leadership team we take them through a handful of steps to enable them to zoom in on the specific behaviors that matter. If you are doing this on your own, you can follow these steps:

If we jumped right in and listed one of your company's goals in the left column, then asked, "What behaviors do we need to achieve that goal?" Most likely, we'd see a room full of blank faces. "What behaviors do we want?" is a difficult question to answer in a way that feels useful.

With that in mind, we will start where it is easiest. At this point we are going to invert the organization chart for most companies. At the top of the inverted organization chart are all the people who are customer-facing employees. These people could be service people, sales people, finance folks, etc. The easiest behavior for most leaders to describe is how they want their employees to behave with their customers.

The best way to capture these behaviors is to meet in a room with a white board and capture every behavior that comes to mind for how you want your people to behave with customers. Go around the table to get input from everyone[12].

Do no editing at this point, no discussion. Once everyone has said what they want to say, then proceed through a process we call "Purge, Pair, or Preserve." Purge means the item doesn't belong on the list, and we cross it out. Pair means that two items are actually the same thing and should be paired together. Sometime three or four things turn out to be the same thing and they all get 'paired'. We draw an arrow between paired items. Preserve refers to all the items on the list you want to keep. In the first round of Purge Pair or Preserve, be generous and don't purge unless everyone agrees it should go. The most senior person in the room should always speak up last. Pair when it is clear that the items are substantially the same.

---

[12] We recommend you first ask everyone to write down and prioritize their points independently. When capturing items on the white boards, we want each person to give us their top priority item first. If it is already on the white board, then get the person's next highest priority until everyone's list is exhausted.

Examples of customer facing behaviors:
- Know your stuff
- Be polite
- Use good phone etiquette
- The customer is always right
- Be the expert
- Listen!
- Take control of the conversation
- Be succinct
- Be courteous
- Smile
- Understand the customer's problem
- …

After completing the Purge, Pair or Preserve process, have everyone individually pick their top 5 behaviors and rank them by giving the most important a score of 5 points; the next most important gets a score of 4; etc. Record the scores from everyone on the white board. Sum the scores where people ranked the same behavior. Then take the top five and put them in the first box under 'Supporting Behaviors'. In the 'Key Company Attributes' column write, "Customer-facing behaviors".

Next you follow the same exercise to identify the behaviors you never want to see an employee engage in when dealing with a customer. You may have more fun here. When you Purge, Pair, or Preserve this list do the purging and pairing aggressively. The banned behaviors should be short and provide reasonable guidelines.

Examples of customer-facing banned behaviors:
- Never lose your temper with a customer.
- Never hang up on a customer.
- Never lie to a customer.

- Never be rude.
- Never be sarcastic
- Never assume you know what the customer wants.
- …

Score these in the same way you scored the desired behaviors and add the top five to the box under the 'Banned Behaviors' heading.

This first exercise helps get the juices rolling.

Competitive Advantage

Next we are going to look at the business results we want. We will approach this from two angles. This will help us zoom in on behaviors that matter most to the company.

First, each person on the leadership team makes a list of up to five ways your company creates competitive advantage[13]. This can be many different kinds of things. Start by thinking how you compete. "We compete on quality", or "Price is our competitive advantage", or "We give high-touch customer service". We take companies through a quick process to identify their unique sources of competitive advantage. If you choose to do this on your own, capture each person's input on a white board, have them rank their top 4 items and calculate the top four for the group.

Take the top four and define the behaviors that support each of them. If it is 'Low costs', you might have a behavior that precludes customization, or one that focuses on least cost. Famously, at Southwest Airlines low costs are a way of life. One behavior Southwest Airlines uses to support this is rapid

---

[13] By itself, this exercise can be quite revealing. If you have very different perspectives, it would be worthwhile to have a separate discussion to get everyone on the same page.

gate turnaround. They work hard to get the plane unloaded, serviced and reloaded for the next flight in 20 minutes. (Sartain and Finney 2003)

Southwest also distinguishes itself as a fun airline. That too, is part of its competitive advantage. The flight crews can have fun; however, not in ways that slow down the turn-around of the plane. For example, on Southwest Airlines it is great to celebrate the co-pilot's birthday. But don't throw confetti. Why? Because cleaning up the confetti takes time and will require extra steps in the cleaning process. The extra steps will slow down the turnaround time for the next flight. It serves one competitive advantage -- having fun, while undermining the other – fast gate turnaround. Therefore throwing confetti is not a desirable behavior.

In our process we would not get as detailed as defining whether or not confetti was allowed, but we would want to link behaviors that support one competitive advantage in order to ensure those behaviors do not undermine other aspects of competitive advantage. This process takes only a little bit of time and can be revised easily as you gain experience with behaviors.

Differentiators

The next step requires you to determine what distinguishes you from your competition in your customers' minds. Your customers choose to buy from you rather than from the competition for some small set of reasons. You need to discover what those are. They may turn out to be things already listed on the chart about how you create competitive advantage. But likely there will also be new things. Use a similar process of capturing and scoring each individual's thoughts to come to three or four top items[14]. Then decide what behaviors support those differentiators. It is obvious that you want behaviors that enhance customers' perceptions of the value of the things you do.

For example: Consumers choose Costco because of the low prices and the high quality of its products. And they choose Method Cleaning Products because Method's products work well and do no harm to the local and global ecosystem. Likewise consumers choose Apple computers because they are well designed and work better than other computers.

Company Goals

We also look at broad goals of the company. These may include revenue, cost control, inventory control, innovation, growth, etc. Go through a similar exercise to identify the desired and banned behaviors around each goal. These too go on the grid.

Lastly, you want to ask, "Are there any additional behaviors that need to be added to the list?" Add any that will contribute to the success of the company.

That completes your first cut at the behavioral grid. Before you roll this out to your employees, you will first complete the other components of the behavioral model.

Roll Out

A *Peer-to-Peer Accountability* group consists of the unit's peer level employees and the manager. (Generally the manager plays a participatory role in these efforts. That is, the manager avoids being the decision-maker as much as possible.)

---

[14] If you discover you have enough variance in how people see the company through the eyes of the customer, you will likely benefit from implementing the Entrepreneurial Operating System described in Gino Wickman's book *Traction*.

The general behavioral grid will be a helpful guide. You will utilize the *Peer-to-Peer Accountability* group to define the desired and banned behaviors for each member of the peer group for the specific role the member plays. This is a one-by-one exercise, focusing on one person at a time.

In this exercise the members of the team, along with the manager and the employee whose position is the subject of the effort, work together to discover and define the needed behaviors. The order of the steps we go through to get there are slightly different from the order described above.

- Identify the 'customers' for this position (internal & external)
- Define customer-facing desired/banned behaviors
- Define the position goals and desired/banned behaviors to achieve the goals.
- Define how this position impacts competitive advantage and what behaviors support that.
- Define how this position creates distinguishers in the eyes of customers and define desired and banned behaviors.

This will likely be an iterative process at first. As your groups get experience doing this, they will get faster and more effective in defining behaviors for members of the peer group.

Once the group has settled on the needed behaviors they are added to the Colleague Letter of Commitments (CLC). We will talk about the CLC in the chapter on Structure

People tend to deliver what is asked of them, particularly when what is needed is clear. Getting the right behavior does not, by itself, maximize the value of the employee. For that, we need to get the person highly motivated.

Motivation

The other day I was walking around a piece of land with a couple of people who want to create a community garden in our town. They were asking for my advice, as I'd previously run a community garden. At one point we were looking at some donated buckets of different kinds of fertilizers. One of the people was a retired PhD chemist and an expert in fertilizer. He stuck a weathered hand into a bucket, picked up a handful of fertilizer and lovingly let the grains fall through his fingers back into the bucket. Clearly, he had respect and affection for the stuff. He would clap his hands across one another, knocking off the remaining bits of fertilizer into the bucket. "This is Urea 21%," he would announce. When he'd identified all the buckets this way, he looked at me. "I'm a chemist by training. You know why I chose to work in fertilizers?" he asked. I shrugged. "I have no idea," I replied. He looked me, his eyes sparkling, and with great seriousness said, "World peace!"

He then went on to explain that fertilizer and better growing techniques have boosted the capacity of soil to produce food. This greatly increases the world's ability to feed people. He went on to say, "Wars start when one group has plenty and their neighbors go hungry. Fertilizer means more for everyone, and one less reason to go to war." I didn't have a counter argument, nor would I have presented one if I did. His work was saving lives by enabling people to live peacefully with one another. He'd found passion for his work. I thought, "What a lucky man!"

This is how you want your people to feel about the company, and the work they. They need to share a sense of intrinsic goodness (Clark and Flagg 2007). In this chapter we will talk about motivating your people. However, it is really about putting in place structures that keep you from demotivating them. People are self-motivated.

Five years after his father's death in 1930, Kiichiro Toyoda and members of the Toyoda (Toyota) management team announced a set of five precepts that had defined his father, Sakichi's, approach to business. They remain a part of Toyota's Way today: (Toyota 2012)

1. Be contributive to the development and welfare of the country by working together, regardless of position, in faithfully fulfilling your duties;
2. Be at the vanguard of the times through endless creativity, inquisitiveness and pursuit of improvement;
3. Be practical and avoid frivolity;
4. Be kind and generous, strive to create a warm, homelike atmosphere; and
5. Be reverent, and show gratitude for things great and small in thought and deed.

When Toyoda said, "create a warm, homelike atmosphere" he meant it literally. Sakichi would often come to the factory early on cold mornings to light the fire in the stoves to warm the building before other team members arrived for work.

The easiest way to get to the intrinsic good in what you do is to use another Sakichi Toyoda tool called the "5 Why's". Start by stating what your company does. Then ask this question: "Why does what we do matter?" And then to the answer of that first question, ask: "Why does that matter?" And so on until you get to the intrinsic good that needs no explanation, when the answer is: "Because it does." It should be an intrinsic good that many people can easily align with their own need to create *Meaning* in their lives.

Core Ideology

The first piece you need to put into place for strong motivation has to do with how employees relate to the company. The key here is your explicit Core Ideology. Jim Collins and Jerry Porras in *Built to Last* describe the notion of Core Ideology. Core Ideology consists of your Core Values and your Core Purpose. Thus, the first step is to define Core Purpose.

Of course the fundamental purpose of a for-profit business is to make a profit. But making money for someone else does not inspire most people. One company's Core Purpose read like this:

> *"The purpose of the _____ Company is to earn money for its shareholders and increase the value of their investment. We will do that through growing the company, controlling assets and properly structuring the balance sheet, thereby increasing EPS, cash flow, and return on invested capital."*[15]

---

[15] As reported at http://www.missionstatements.com But we redacted the company's name because on the company's website their mission statement is much different.

It would be hard for most employees to find a basis for creating personal *Meaning* from a statement like this.

The Purpose we are after is one that allows our employees to create *Meaning*. In *Built to Last*, Collins and Porras give many examples of how companies define their core purpose. We want to ensure that the core purpose contains some intrinsic good. For example, in our company the underlying motivation for doing the work we do is to make our client's workplace healthier, happier, and a place where people are eager to come to work. By accomplishing this, we make the world a better place. It is a worthwhile purpose and it energizes us as colleagues in our enterprise. Additionally, we explicitly make a purpose of our business to have fun together.

Once you have established your Purpose you will decide if you need to add any Core Values to the equation.

We differ from Collins and Porras when it comes to core values because their model links core values to behavioral guides. Often under the *Built to Last* model and subsequent models you will see values that have nothing to do with an intrinsic good. As a consequence many of the core values that companies create under this model are nothing more than very broad, and largely useless behavior statements. Values like: *Innovate don't imitate*, or *We are committed to great products*, or *We are efficient and effective* do not contain intrinsic good and are targeted toward behaviors.

Because we explicitly deal with behaviors in a much more robust way, and because values do not actually guide behavior, we are going to look to values to help us motivate our desired behaviors. Thus, each value we look for must answer the 'how' question: "How do we go about delivering our Purpose?" This 'how' must directly link to an intrinsic good.

Sometimes your Core Purpose statement says it all. Typically the Core Purpose statement answers the *What We Do* and *Why We Do It* questions (see the chapter on Structure). If you need to answer the *How We Do It* question then do so with your Core Values. Method Cleaning Products makes effective products for the home because clean is healthy. That is their Core Purpose. Method augments their Core Purpose with a couple of intrinsically good *How* statements. They make their products completely environmentally friendly, both what's inside and what's outside. In addition to being non-toxic to the environment, their products are non-toxic to the humans who use them. These are two intrinsically good *How* statements: friendly to the environment, and non-toxic to humans, round out their Core Ideology.

Behavior Aligned Values

In thinking about values statements that deal with the *How* there are three other workplace factors that could be addressed. The first is fairness.

Fairness

The single most important management aspect of motivation is not how to motivate employees, but rather how to avoid de-motivating employees. When employees talk about management it is often in a negative context. It is the negative aspects of management that get people excited.

For example, think about 'fairness'. People generally don't get excited when they are treated fairly. What gets people excited is when they are treated unfairly. We generally do not talk about fairness unless there is some worry about unfairness. Fairness doesn't motivate people, but unfairness certainly impacts motivation. How people feel about a company is impacted by fairness inside the company.

Everything we do, we do with the intention to be fair: fair to each other, fair to customers, fair to suppliers, and fair to stockholders.

Human beings seem to have a deeply ingrained sense of fairness. It usually appears most strongly around situations where potential loss is involved. If a company runs into financial trouble the employees generally understand a cutback in salaries and a hiring freeze. However, if the burden is not shared in a way that feels fair, then people will find ways to get revenge. This is human nature.

For example: Shortly after the recession hit in 2008, a Chicago based Fortune 500 company announced a layoff of 500 people. This number represented a rather small portion of the workforce. This was a firm that consistently ran in fourth place among four large competitors. The CEO justified the cuts saying it had to be done to "put our business in the strongest possible position going forward." At the employee town-hall someone asked if they had looked at other alternatives to a layoff like taking a salary reduction. The executive responded that some senior executives we going to see cuts as high as 50% of their compensation. That sounded like a lot. Here is what the senior guys' prior year compensation looked like.

Executive Position	Salary
CEO	$21,700,000
President	$17,900,000
EVP Customer Service	$ 7,700,000
EVP CIO	$ 7,600,000
CFO	$ 7,600,000
Total	$62,500,000

In this case a 50% cut would leave the five executives to divide up over $30 million.

The executive compensation was published in a local paper. Employees are not oblivious to information like this. The issue around fairness is rarely expressed as a positive. It surfaces when something is unfair. In this case morale in the firm suffered dramatically. Today, the senior team in this firm make less than a tenth of the numbers above and it remains secure in its fourth place spot. It will take time for this company to fully recover.

Having an empathetic sense of fairness is a trait of a good leader. If you act in ways that are seen as unfair, you undermine your ability to motivate the workforce. You can get people to exhibit the behavior you want, but they are only going through the motions. The parties that get hurt by this are stockholders.

Management has far more potential to demotivate employees than to motivate them. This is similar to the impact generals can have on the success of soldiers in battle. When General Wesley Clark worked at the U.S. Army's National Training Center, he observed that the incoming battalions never beat the smaller resident "enemy," and he wondered why. By observing the fighting, he realized that the resident enemy reacted and fought at the individual soldier level. For the visiting army, all the strategy and tactics were managed through the chain of command. The frontline lieutenants were given a set of tactical instructions and expected to execute the tasks as commanded. The visiting soldiers simply followed whatever reasonable orders were given.

The training center's resident enemy received no such detailed tactical instruction. Their job was simple: to defeat the incoming army by whatever means necessary. It was the initiative and ingenuity of the frontline soldier that made the difference in the outcome of the battle. The frontline soldiers worked in small teams; defined the problem they faced at any moment; and invented a solution. They were free to behave as thinking adults. This is why the smaller resident enemy always won the battle.

What General Clark realized was the actions of senior commanders could lose a battle, but their orders could not win it. In much the same way as the winning initiative and ingenuity comes from the front line soldier, the winning behavior and motivation comes from the front line employee. Like generals who are wise to stay out of the way of battlefield initiative and ingenuity, business leaders are wise to stay out of the way when it comes to employee motivation. We will hit this idea hard when we talk about leadership.

In the introductory chapter I mentioned the letter from Jonah who works in an economic consulting firm that provides economic studies to law firms. In the letter Jonah describes how he and his fellow consultants routinely overstate their billable hours. Jonah goes on to explain that there are no clear policy guidelines as to what behavior is acceptable. But it is clear to him and his colleagues that over-billing is what's expected.

Management is happy because the bill gets passed on to the law firm, which happily marks up the price and passes it on to their client. The only people that seem unhappy about this are Jonah and his colleagues. They are required to lie about their billable hours. They do it but, as Jonah's discomfort indicates, it bothers them. You can imagine that the published values of Jonah's firm do not include, "We will cheat every customer." Perhaps the clearest guideline came when the solitary consultant, who refused to inflate his billable hours, got laid off. The message was clear; don't do what he did.

In my consulting practice I occasionally hear about scenarios like this. The other day, when I met with my Wednesday morning group, one of the attorneys in the group was complaining about a law firm he competes with; and one lawyer in particular who will bill out 24 hours in a day. He also said that at the end of every month the managing partner spends two days calling in each of the firm's lawyers for a two minute update on each of their clients. Each client gets billed for 15 minutes (the minimum billing increment) of the managing partner's time. For the managing partner these 15 minute increments add up. In fact, these questionable 15 minute billings are so numerous that they make the managing partner the highest revenue generator in the firm. You can easily imagine similar irregular scenarios playing out in thousands of law firms, accounting firms, consulting firms, and any other firm where customers pay for billable hours.

The case of Jonah's economic analysis firm is a good example of how a company failed to structure itself in a way that protected its workforce from a strong de-motivator. While the psychological research is convincing that values do not regulate behavior, it is also clear that when we are asked to do something that violates our values, we feel demotivated. We may behave in the manner dictated, but we will behave unenthusiastically.

In the law firm case mentioned above, you can imagine how a young lawyer feels when called in to talk to the managing partner. The young lawyer is responsible for the relationship with the client and he knows that every month when he mentions that client to the managing partner, the firm will cheat the client a little bit. To the young lawyer it might seem underhanded, petty, and unsavory, and would likely be demoralizing as a result.

These kinds of leadership behaviors undermine the potential extra effort you'd like to see in your employees.

Adding a value around fairness can help ensure that unfair actions by the management team do not negatively impact employees and ultimately stockholders.

No Politics Please! We're a community.

We care about one another, we don't engage in politics, we are open and honest and never talk behind someone's back.

Belonging to a community is a natural human need. Establish an environment where a community can thrive. Fundamentally in a healthy community people do not talk behind each other's backs. This is particularly important for Behavioral Advantage™ because gossiping undermines the social structure that enables *Peer-to-Peer Accountability* . We must like and respect our peers to feel accountable to them for our behavior. To like and respect someone, you must first trust him or her. Ultimately, you want everyone who works at the company to feel as though they are an important member of the company community. You will install a mechanism that supports and open and honest dialogue, where issues are addressed and resolved with a positive candid discussion.

Autonomy

We trust everyone to do the job they've agreed to perform. They don't need to be managed.

If you do a good job of structuring the job and defining the right behaviors, then you should not need to micro-manage the behavior in the job.

Once you have established your "What We Do", "Why We Do It", and "How We Do It" statements you can have some fun articulating them and bringing them to life to make them tangible for your workforce. Freely abandon any structure around answering the three questions. Articulate with abandon! Tell a story. Have some fun. The output should be stimulating to you and your people. Take a look at how Method Company handles this on their website. Go to: http://methodhome.com/#

click on "Methodology" in the upper right of the page. Clearly, they did not follow a consultant's format for doing this, it is absolutely original.

Engagement

The right behavior is good. The right behavior, strongly motivated, is great. This is popularly described as having 'fully-engaged' employees. Most literature about engagement describes the *what* of engagement and the *value* of engagement to the organization. There is less material around how to create or enable this engagement.

Companies like Right Management, for example, do a good job of determining the level of engagement in a company. They will benchmark a business for a client, enabling them to know where they stand relative to other companies. The surveys will categorize the employees into groups by level of engagement: Fully Engaged, Engaged, Unengaged, and Disengaged. Companies like Right look at the various elements that go into determining the level of engagement. They will work with the management team on refining the *what* behind that engagement with the goal of identifying the two or three critical areas that the company needs to focus on.

In our experience, you do not need to conduct a survey to know whether or not you have fully engaged employees. If you pay attention, it's obvious. Why benchmarking engagement levels is important is also a mystery. Perhaps there is comfort in knowing that your company is above average when it comes to engagement. 'Above average' is a mediocre position to take; especially when it's possible to fully engage your entire workforce.

If you want some kind of measure of engagement, for example to measure progress, you can measure the aggregate responses to this question: *"On a scale of 1 to 10, how likely is it that you would recommend our company as a place of employment to a qualified friend or colleague?"* This is very similar to Bain & Company's Net Promoter® Score. When the score isn't as high as you'd expect, you may get additional insight by asking a question that Bain & Company says yields a more complete gauge of the health of employees' faith in the company. It goes something like this, *"On a scale of 1 to 10 how likely is it that you would recommend our products or services to a friend or colleague?"*

Numerous companies can help you survey your employees to measure their level of engagement. These companies will analyze the results and give you direction on how to boost your levels of engagement. Each one of these companies attempts to address employee engagement with wide strokes, as though engagement factors are consistent across individuals in the employee population. It is analogous to trying to fix an out of balance condition on your books by only looking only at the totals. The error is going to be at the individual transactions level. You can't fix the errors looking only at the account totals. This is also true when it comes to engagement. It is always the individual employee who is either fully engaged or not.

Typically the promise these firms make is that they will <u>raise</u> the level of engagement in the company. They don't suggest that 100% of employees could be fully engaged; rather they expect some employees to become fully engaged while most remain under-engaged. Think about this: teams of fully engaged employees outperform all other teams by 240%. (Van Allen 2009, 11) If you had a company of 1000 employees and 27% of them were fully engaged, then you'd have 730 employees who were not. Why would a company want to pay these 730 people if they weren't fully engaged? Does the company leadership believe that on the whole planet, there are only 270 people who could be fully engaged in the work they do? Or is it that their leadership and the consultants they've engaged, simply don't know how to engage the entire workforce? After all, this isn't something you learn in your MBA program.

Engagement comes from within the individual employee. The idea of tailoring to the individual is a key concept in Behavioral Advantage™ ™. We strive to make that as easy as possible and thereby enable you to have 100% of your employees fully engaged.

Much of the foundation for this work is based on psychological studies and insights. As such, we recognize that psychology is a phenomenological science. Psychological theories rarely operate like theories in physics. In physics, a theory must be predictive in 100% of cases. In psychology, you rarely achieve that level of confidence. We love any psychological theory that is predictive 90% of the time. That still means one in ten times it is wrong. Thus, in focusing on the individual, we recognize that fairly often the answer for one person will be different from the answer for another. The answer matters because without it, you do not fully engage the employee.

The Value of Engagement

Gallup surveys estimate the value of engagement from time to time. For example: a pre-recession Gallup report said, "business units high in employee engagement… nearly triple their chances for above-average success across business units in all companies." (Harter, et al. 2009, 32) We take it as widely accepted that paying motivated employees is better than paying unmotivated employees. If you are paying the salary of an employee who isn't fully engaged, you're throwing money away. 100% of your employees should be fully engaged, no excuses.

Many companies correlate employee engagement levels to financial metrics such as gross margin, profit, revenues, and shareholder value. Aon Hewitt reported that "organizations with high levels of engagement (65% or greater) … posted total shareholder returns 22% higher than average in 2010." (AON Hewitt 2012) Towers Watson reports that companies with high employee engagement enjoy operating margins three time larger than those with low employee engagement. (Towers Watson 2012) (Presumably the engagement level cause the financial performance, and not the other way around.) In these studies there were pockets of full engagement, however, not all employees were fully engaged. The 240% results reported on a previous page were from teams comprised entirely of fully engaged employees.

We think the evidence that full employee engagement has tremendous value to a firm is convincing. Since you're still reading, chances are you agree.

Who is Responsible?

Ultimately, who is responsible for the employee's engagement: the employee, or management? There are three schools of thought concerning this.

1. In a hierarchical organization the power and authority of the manager gives the manager extraordinary influence on the employee's state of mind and emotional condition. Certainly where a manager behaves like a jerk, this is true. Most of us with a few years of work experience have had a boss like this.[16] When one of these jerks walks into the room, the energy walks out.

2. It is the employee who takes responsibility for their own engagement. Interestingly, the evidence supporting this position comes from asking highly engaged employees "Who is responsible for your

---

[16] Stanford professor Robert Sutton has written a fun book about this problem called *The No Asshole Rule*.

engagement level?" These employees claim that responsibility. Disengaged employees tend to blame their manager and the work environment. Both positions seem to be a bit self-serving.

3. Responsibility for engagement is a mix of the employee, his or her peers, and their management. We subscribe to this view and have built our tools to leverage all three groups, with the peer group playing the key role.

Engagement How-To

This is a 'How To' book; thus we will be talking about how you can get highly motivated, right behaviors from everyone.

A leader's role in an organization is to get the right behavior and to ensure the motivators are working at full steam. In studying motivation there are many different ways to classify motivators. We chose to make it simple: there are two kinds of motivators at work – ones that lend themselves to scorekeeping and ones that don't.

Scorekeeping

One type of motivator lends itself to scorekeeping and typically only produces short term results.

The trouble with motivators that allow for scorekeeping is that you are either motivating or demotivating. It's a hill-climb. You're going up; then you're going down. When we talk about engagement we don't want people to be fully engaged one day, disengaged the next, and then engaged again a day later. We realize that such swings would ultimately result in a much less-engaged workforce.

Years ago the Securities and Exchange Commission decided they needed to reign in executive compensation. Thinking that public exposure of the problem would create sufficient outrage that companies would put the brakes on, the SEC required companies to publish how much they paid their senior executives. Unfortunately, it backfired. The publishing of executive pay made it much easier to keep score. Because scorekeeping is an escalating enterprise, executive compensation took another leap upward soon after the regulation took effect.

For many other people, money affords them the opportunity to keep score publicly: they buy bigger homes; more cars; etc. When that happens, a given quantity of money does not sustain motivation. You need more.

A few people are able reach a point where they have enough money; it no longer motivates. A couple of years ago a CEO of a commercial insurance brokerage called us in. His sales force exasperated him. He'd grown his business by acquiring other smaller, successful, well established insurance brokers. He wanted to leverage the acquired sales force to grow the business organically. Unfortunately the company did not grow as he'd hoped. He discovered that every salesperson he'd acquired was making more money than he or she ever expected to make. They felt no need to go out and aggressively seek new customers. Each salesperson had a set of customers that they kept happy by hosting golf outings. A few new customers did trickle in through customer referrals; unfortunately, this only kept pace with natural customer attrition.

This CEO's motivational model was based entirely on money. Such motivational models work only up to the point where the incremental cost equals the incremental return. Beyond that point, more money simply has no motivational value.

The value of money can be hard to predict from a motivational perspective. You get a very nice bonus and are very happy until you discover that the lazy S.O.B. sitting next to you who plays tennis with the boss got 5% more than you did. Suddenly you feel demotivated.

Non-Scorekeeping

The second type of motivators does not easily lend itself to scorekeeping and delivers sustainable results. For that reason we want to focus on motivators that deliver sustainable results. In that context, we will avoid motivators that lend themselves to scorekeeping.

We want to be very clear here and avoid any confusion between motivation and behavior. Our structure is based on defining behavior. We've already discussed this. We don't use motivation to determine <u>what</u> behavior we get. Instead, we define the behavior we want, and use motivation to put the juice behind that behavior.

It is a bit like the difference between what we do and how much we do it. In this case, behavior defines what we do; while motivation defines how much energy and thought we put into that behavior. You could argue that motivated behavior is a type of behavior, and you'd be right. We make the distinction because Milgram and others have shown us people will produce the behavior we want when we set the right context. However, in our case, that is not enough. We want them to feel driven to do the behaviors and be personally invested in those behaviors.

Motivation is simply our ability to tap into what is already there. To get the best out of our people we cannot expect to motivate them without ensuring that the behaviors we ask for are consistent and compatible with their personal values.

We have already talked about how values link to behavior. If we are asked to behave in a manner that conflicts with our values we will feel uncomfortable. We won't like it. We will feel like we are accomplishing one thing while undermining another. It drains enthusiasm. We will execute the behavior, but without energy.

While the psychological research is convincing that values do not govern behavior, it is also clear that when we are asked to do something that violates our values we feel demotivated. We behave in the manner dictated; however, we behave unenthusiastically.

Recall Jonah, the analyst in the economic consulting firm where they overstated billable hours. Jonah's firm could have structured itself differently and achieved the same economic result. The firm provides value to its customer and needs to be paid for that value. Some of that value is built into the pre-existing knowledge and capabilities of the analysts and managers. How the company bills for services is independent from what it requires its analyst to report internally. Internally analysts can be evaluated based on the quality of their work. I started my career as an analyst. The number of hours an analyst works on an analysis is hard to measure anyway. If analysts are highly motivated they will be working through the analysis all the time: when they are in the shower, on the golf course, and even when they are sleeping, their brains will be problem solving and analyzing. Jonah's company could have structured the work such that the analysts take great pride in their work rather than feel they are working dishonestly. The firm could have recognized that the actual hours reported does not accurately reflect the problem solving activity going on in the analysts' brains, even when they are not in the office. The firm could have structured billing to customers differently and removed the demotivating 'requirement' to cheat.

This brings us to one other observation about motivators. Some values only surface in a de-motivational environment. For example, fairness. We value fairness. However, a fair environment doesn't create motivation for us, whereas an unfair environment can demotivate us. The same is true of gossip. An environment where gossip is not present does not provide us with motivation. People talking behind our backs can be demotivating.

We will focus on the things that get us motivated. Ultimately you want to define the right behaviors and then energize those behaviors by linking their outcomes to the employee's ability to create self-motivation. The concept of self-motivation brings us to a key concept. We talk here about motivating employees. It is the common way we talk about this subject. But it is not really about how to motivate employees. It is about how to stop doing the things that demotivate employees. Employees are already motivated, we just need to avoid blocking what already motivates each employee. Our focus on certain things will enable us to behave in ways that don't step on these motivators.

AIMS Model

Before we zoom in on how you will motivate your employees (or stop demotivating them), we want to give you one more foundational block. We do that by introducing a motivational model called the AIMS[17] Model. It consists of four categories of motivators: Appetites, *Identity*, *Meaning*, and Sex (AIMS).

---

[17] From psychologists Abraham Maslow, B.F. Skinner, and Frederick Herzberg, to research by behavioral economists like Daniel Kahneman, and Daniel Ariely we have a wealth of insights into human motivators. More recently we've seen an effort to pull these different tracks into a more unified model. This effort attempts to consolidate four theories into a single model. These four are:

Theory of Picoeconomics - Humans have an innate tendency to undervalue future events. We tend to put off tasks leading to distant valuable goals in favor of ones with immediate but lesser value.

Category	Descriptors
Appetites	Our desire for things: goods, food, drink, health, happiness, well-being
Identity	How we want others to see us: reputation, position, rank, influence, esteem, fame, prestige, standing, and character.
Meaning	Things that have meaning to us personally: accomplishment, self-creation, problem solving, the sense of mastery, and doing good.
Sex	Our deep needs for constituent security and connection with other people: love, friendship, family, belonging, jealousy, power, guilt, and, of course, sex.

The AIMS model is a 'needs theory' model. Needs theories state that behaviors are driven by needs. Let's review these categories in more detail.

Appetites

Companies address Appetites by paying their employees and providing benefits. We will not focus on these as motivators partly because they tend to be transient and/or unpredictable. Additionally, because Appetites are quantifiable, they lend

---

Expectancy theory - For each option before us, our brains take in two considerations: First, what is the probability that this outcome will be achieved; and second, how much is the expected outcome valued?

CPT - Choices made are based on outcomes defined as possible losses and possible gains. Losses loom larger than gains and probabilities tend to converge to the center. We are loss averse.

Need theories - Behaviors are driven by needs. We pursue actions that most reduce our strongest need. We also pursue actions that provide the most utility.

For the purposes of work environment structure the AIMS needs theory is sufficient. However, Kahneman's work is worth incorporating into policy development. Fundamentally, how we dialogue with one another, and how we deal with risk will greatly impact our ability to tap the highest needs of *Identity* and Meaning.

themselves to scorekeeping. Appetites tend to be needs and desires that change rapidly and escalate easily. People compare income, houses, cars, and lifestyles with their peers, superiors, neighbors, friends, and family. The natural tendency is for more, more, more; better, better, better.

Motivational programs based on Appetites lose their power fairly quickly because people take things for granted once they have them. A great example of this phenomenon is in how people view perquisites. People tend to value perks most when they are excluded from them. Once they achieve the level to receive those perks, the perks quickly become entitlements. Once someone feels they are entitled to something, it loses much of its motivational power.

When you allow an appetite like making money to become your company's primary motivator you will run into this problem.

A friend of ours in a technology company hired a technologist away from a competitor by offering him more money. This employee had worked for a handful of other companies over the last four years. At our friend's company he lasted less than nine months. It turned out that this fellow's first employer focused on money as the key motivator. Employees within that company learned to measure their self-worth based on the size of their salary. As a consequence, when a outside offer came along for more money he saw it as increasing his self-worth and he jumped ship. He ended up changing jobs four more times in the next three years, each time for more money. It should have come as no surprise to our friend's company that motivating this individual through his appetite for more money would end the way it did. When self-worth gets linked to a scorekeeping mechanism, there is no such thing as 'enough'.

We recently met with a senior partner at a large, local law firm. They wanted to talk with us because they are worried about losing their best young lawyers. In law firms the partners own shares in the business that entitle them to portions of the firm's profits. This means that the lower ranked lawyers share a smaller pie irrespective of how much new business they bring in. This firm has a handful of young rainmakers and they are worried about losing them over the issue of self-worth. The amount of each employee's compensation is known by all members in the firm. It is how people are measured by others and how they measure themselves. This problem is exacerbated by the firm's unwillingness to talk about people's values in other terms, e.g. *Identity* and *Meaning*. The members of the firm worry that if they say something positive about a colleague's legal expertise, or the great way they deal with clients, or their legal creativity, then they will immediately demand more money; and the pie is only so big. They want us to show them a way out of this quandary.

Scorekeeping is a poor way to determine your employees' self-worth. The only way to avoid this is to redefine how employees determine their sense of self-worth. That's what this chapter is about. We will <u>not</u> focus on appetites as motivators. Clearly you have to pay your people well enough and provide them competitive benefits or these things could become demotivators.

<u>Sex</u>
'S' is for Sex. In the AIMS model we are not really talking about sex. We're actually talking about Relationships. But the acronym needed an 'S' and 'Sex' is,... more eye catching, plus it whenever we mention it, we always get a smile.

What we are referring to with Relationships is our need for companionship, love, friendship, power, etc. Oddly enough, like Appetites, Relationships can lend themselves to scorekeeping. People want to be the most popular, the most loved, the favorite son, etc. Relationships matter for us, hence they are a source of motivation. However, trying to leverage this motivator in a business context is akin to walking through a minefield; you end up with a highly political environment, which tends to undermine other motivators.

You do not have to focus on this motivator for a different reason. Your people's need for healthy relationships is easily and naturally fulfilled when the motivational structure introduced here is implemented. When employees participate in enabling co-workers to create the *Identity* they want and find the *Meaning* they need in the work they do, then natural relationships form. Additionally, the structure you will put in place will cause employees to resolve misbehaviors, emotional outbursts, and other potentially damaging interactions before they can fester. Good, positive and useful relationships flourish in this environment.

To motivate your employees you will focus on the other two aspects of the AIMS model: *Identity* and *Meaning*. These two motivators do not easily lend themselves to scorekeeping. They persist as motivators because we root them in things that will not easily change. As long as we create the right conditions, then *Identity* and *Meaning* will retain their power to motivate forever.

Identity

Identity is how we want others to see us. We may have different *Identities* in different social contexts. In our homes we have one *Identity*; in the community a different one; at work another *Identity*; and at our alma mater perhaps even another one. Across individuals the *Identity* we want may differ greatly, depending upon what matters most to us.

It is crucial for every one of our employees to be able to establish a worthy *Identity*. Behaviors impact that *Identity*, as do other things like authority, position, structure, status, and how we interact with one another. Status is an important element. In the US Army a Corporal is the second lowest rank[18]. The army endows the rank of Corporal with status. The rank is a leadership rank. The Army describes the NCO corps (Non Commissioned Officer) as the backbone of the Army, and the Corporal as the backbone of the NCO corps. When you become a Corporal you establish *Identity* for which you can rightfully be proud. (Although it is the Army, so there's plenty to complain about!)

One of our colleagues worked with a team leader named Joe, who'd worked hard to establish the *Identity* of a project leader who could deliver results. One day an interested senior manager noticed Joe seemed more distant than usual and less enthusiastic. When she sat down with Joe to talk about it, Joe repeatedly dodged questions, and seemed uncomfortable with the conversation. Later a co-worker shed light on the problem. Joe's direct manager had taken the title of 'project leader' from Joe and given it to himself since the project fell under his domain. The manager did not play an active role in the project; however, as the 'project leader' he would officially received credit for the work even though Joe, was the brains and hands behind the execution. This stripped Joe of *Identity* as project leader. It was an *Identity* that Joe had carefully cultivated.

Fortunately, this was a simple problem to fix. The title of 'project leader' was returned to Joe, he came back up to his normal level of performance.

Identity isn't only about individual *Identity*. We also have group *Identity*. The nature of our group's *Identity* can have significant influence on behavior and motivation. It is part of the herd effect. Dan Ariely tells an illuminating and humorous story about the power of group *Identity* over behavior. He says that

---

[18] On a pay grade basis, the Corporal is the 4th lowest pay grade in the army. Below the corporal are two Private pay grades and a Specialist.

what determines whether a group follows a cheater's example depends upon what kind of sweatshirt the cheater is wearing. The cheating experiment he refers to took place in Pittsburgh at Carnegie Mellon University with Carnegie Mellon students. In the experiment the students had to answer a set of problems that would take some time to solve. They were prepaid and were asked to give back a portion of the money based on how many problems they were not able to solve in the allotted time. As soon as the experiment started a student confederate stood up and declared that he's solved all the problems, and asked what should he do. He was told he could leave with his money. Clearly he was cheating. What impact would his getting away with obvious cheating have on the other students behavior? Here is where the sweatshirt comes into play. If he was wearing a Carnegie Mellon sweatshirt, he was one of the group, and cheating went up. However, if he was wearing a University of Pittsburgh sweatshirt, he represented a different group, and cheating went down.   Clearly group *Identity* influences behavior.

Creating *Identity*

We want to use *Identity* for motivational purposes. To the extent that you can endow every position in the company with overt status, you will enhance your employee's ability to establish a worthy *Identity*. Creating this for new positions is a primary function of the Human Relations[19] department. Absorbing this responsibility will boost the professional contribution of your HR personnel. We will dig into how we set up jobs to accomplish this when we get to the HR chapter.

---

[19] "HR" today is used to stand for Human Resources. We revert back to the earlier meaning - Human Relations. This designation more closely aligns to dealing with people as people rather than as assets. We would also like to distinguish between the role of HR in regulatory compliance and its role to deal with the psychological aspects of working with employees.

Working with the motivational factor of *Identity* led us to one of the most important insights into why existing employee engagement strategies get such mediocre results.

We form our *Identities* in various social contexts: at work; in the community; at our place of worship; in our extended families; in our immediate family; and with our college buddies with whom we occasionally go out to have a beer. When we form these *Identities* we use three different structures. Most *Identities* are created in adult-to-adult relationships. In our immediate

families, part of the *Identity* is Parent-to-Child when we play the parent role to our children and their friends. When we go out with our college buddies, it's a Child-to-Child relationship; we're just having some fun.

However, at no point do we seek out an *Identity* where we play the Child role and some other adult plays the Parent role. This relationship makes us uncomfortable and we don't like it. When it is imposed upon us, we like it even less. The look on the little girl's face in the photo is exactly how we all feel about being in that position. We seek to avoid it.

Unfortunately, the way hierarchical companies structure the manager-to-subordinate relationship, it devolves into a Parent-to-Child relationship far too often. Because the person in the superior position can get some valuable *Identity* for themselves by playing the power card, the lure of the Parent role can be very strong. And even for a good manager, no matter how hard he or she tries to keep the relationship on an Adult-to-Adult level, the subtext for the subordinate is always that this is just a misstep away from going to Parent-to-Child. It is an uncomfortable relationship. Bad managers have taught us this, and we've all met these managers.

Identity is a very strong motivator. If this Child-to-Parent relationship is onerous, then it will have a significant negative impact on *Identity*. That meant we needed to go find data that would confirm or deny this insight.

The first thing we did was ask the question, "Do reasons why people voluntarily leave a company point in this direction?" So we went out and did something foolish. We went to look at exit interview data. There's lots of exit interview data. Fortunately, someone pointed out a small problem with using this data. In exit interviews, 96% of departing employees give a false reason for why they leave. They don't want to burn any bridges. What's the real reason for leaving? It is almost always bad management! (Kreisman 2002)

The idea that people leave managers and not companies has been the subject of numerous articles and books. The data that supports this does suggest that perhaps *Identity* is a key factor here.

We then wanted to find some corroborating data that was significantly different in its source. It was a moment of serendipity that informed me where to look. I saw a photo of Richard Feynman playing the bongo drums. Feynman was a

Nobel Laureate physicist who once wrote a book titled, *What Do You Care What Other People Think*. On the spectrum of people who care about what others think of them (the foundation of *Identity*) Richard Feynman was far down the curve near the end marked 'Doesn't care at all.' We wondered what was at the other end.

Certainly, in every society and culture there are people who care a great deal about what others think of them. But in some cultures it's more pronounced than in others. In countries like China, Korea, Japan, Thailand, and Singapore the concept of 'Saving Face' is prevalent. This concept is a bit alien to those of us who grew up in a western culture. In a western culture, if someone in a group says something a little negative about someone else it generally does not overly influence the opinions of members of the group. And it certainly does not impact the subject's own sense of self worth. However, in a 'Saving Face' culture having something slightly negative said about you will diminish you in the eyes of all who heard the remark, but more interestingly, it will diminish your own sense of self worth.

Putting people from those cultures into a manager-to-subordinate hierarchy would likely have an even bigger negative impact on their sense of *Identity*. That would make motivating and engaging employees in those cultures even more challenging. The question then became, is there data that supports this. Yes there is!

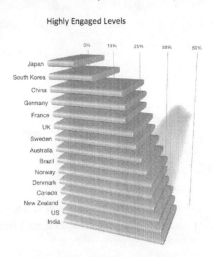

Highly Engaged Levels

This graph is based on data published by Right Management in 2009 (Haid and Sims 2009). As the graph indicated, the countries where the proportion of highly engaged workers is the lowest are Japan, South Korea, and China. They are all countries where the concept of 'Saving Face' is an important part of the culture. The China data is suspect. When you collect employee engagement data you tell the employees that they can answer honestly because the survey is anonymous. That requires a level of trust of authority. Unfortunately in China, people in authority have often not been trustworthy. Thus, it is reasonable to believe the data overstates the real level of engagement in China. It is probably closer to Japan's numbers.

All this points to the simple observation that traditional management structures undermine *Identity* as a key element of motivation. If a company does not address this issue, it will not be successful in getting 100% of employees fully engaged. How can you deal with this relationship issue when the company is built around this very relationship? Fortunately, that's a problem for which a solution already exists. That solution is *Peer-to-Peer Accountability*. All we will need to do is build the structure to enable us to overlay the *Peer-to-Peer Accountability* structure to replace the negative impacts of the Parent-to-Child dynamics in the Manager-to-Subordinate structure. Ultimately we accomplish this through the processes we implement described in the Structure chapter.

To eliminate this relationship obstacle we simply move the ongoing responsibility for ensuring every employee has the opportunity to establish and maintain a valued *Identity* to the peer group We provide clients with a couple of simple tools to make this easy to accomplish.

Peer employees behave in ways that actively enhance, rather than undermine, each other's *Identity*. Peers play the primary role to help the employee build and maintain that treasured *Identity*. This process is a key element of the weekly Rated 10 Meeting. We discuss this type of meeting in the chapter on Structure.

When working with a colleague to help him or her to build and maintain a desired *Identity*, the peer group needs to answer two questions. First you must determine what *Identity* is wanted. Second, you have to figure out how to link the work the employee does to that *Identity*. This is a peer group responsibility.

Identity, like *Meaning*, needs to be explicitly created. You accomplish this by asking the employee and the peer group to think about what kind of reputation the person doing this job would have if they were truly outstanding. Typically, people talk about that reputation in ways that are personally meaningful. This is the reputation the employee will likely desire; and the peer group strives to make it possible for the employee to acquire this *Identity*.

Follow this by asking the employee what expertise is needed for the job. Take for example, a lumberjack who cuts down trees for a living. The person in this job might say they would know all about the dynamics of how a tree responds to different cutting approaches. They might know about maintaining a chainsaw engine, or how to manually sharpen and file the cutting and raking surfaces on the chain, etc.[20] When people are asked to catalogue the knowledge required to do their job, they often discover they have acquired substantial, unique knowledge.

---

[20] While in college principal author here worked for the US Forest Service falling trees. More than 10,000 trees fell to his saw (but all for the health of the forest).

The purpose of this exercise is to establish this unique knowledge as expertise. You want to establish that the person is an authority on these topics. This gives their role standing.

If the position has any rank above the bottom rung, that rank is an area to be exploited for creating *Identity*. If the position is indeed bottom rung, you need to clearly articulate the importance of their job to the overall functioning of the whole company.

In addition, it is useful to allow people to establish a values-based *Identity*. This *Identity* is more closely related to the personality of the individual. This part of *Identity* may be different for each individual in the same job. To spark the thinking around what this might be, here is a list of words you can use in the peer group to start the discussion:

Rebel	Inspired
Maverick	Responsible
Creative Genius	Authority
Care Giver	Steadfast
Thoughtful Coach	Sexy
Leader	Fun Loving
Problem Solver	Faithful
Soothsayer	Conservative
Visionary	Liberal
Adventurer	Religious
Powerful	Curious
Healer	Deep Thinker
Lover	Gregarious
Protector	Loner
Expert	Invulnerable
Nerd	Open
Scientist	Intelligent
Methodical	Crafty
Inspiring	Ingenious

Reliable	Warm
Supportive	Listener
Friendly	Helpful

This discussion should lead from choosing additional elements of *Identity* based on the discussion and linking the work to those elements. This takes a bit of creativity from the group. It is how we create unique *Identity*. Sometimes you can't get this done in just one sitting. We recommend you let this simmer in each person's brain for a few days first.

You can enhance *Identity* by adopting a peer emphasized hierarchy. In this form of hierarchy everyone not in your direct chain-of-command is a colleague or a peer. The only exceptions are the employees in your direct line of leadership. Your superiors and your subordinates make up the only hierarchy in the company from your perspective. Everyone else is a peer. Thus, if you are in the operations group, then everyone in the marketing group is a peer from the Chief Marketing Officer to the Copy Clerk. In a flattened hierarchy organization, you do not have a job title per se. You are know by your *Identity*; the expert in such-and-such, with the important responsibility to do this-and-that.

Maintaining *Identity*
The peer group works hard to establish and maintain this *Identity*. The bulk of this work is done in the weekly Rated 10 Meeting. Each week, on a rotating basis, one peer group member receives the focus of the team supporting that person's motivators of *Identity* and *Meaning*.

On a broader scale the entire company also participates. One way in which the broader company participates brings us back around to culture. Most definitions of company culture only deal with the here-and-now. Wikipedia, for example, defines culture as the organization's: *"values, visions, norms, working language, systems, symbols, beliefs and habits."* However, a broader definition of culture includes key defining moments in the history of the company. These selected moments are told as stories, the legends of the company. They inform the corporate *Identity,* and sustain it.

Likewise, you reinforce an individual's *Identity* by this kind of recognition. Citigroup had a research facility in Marina Del Rey, California. The employees who worked there invented the ATM. They also developed much of security and encryption technology used by the banking community. In the facility was a "Wall of Honor". Each time one of them won a patent a small plaque would be placed on the wall naming the patent and its creator. For most people who create them, patents form a part of their *Identity.* Patents are an official recognition of their creative uniqueness.

Highlighting significant individual achievements that align with an individual's sense of *Identity* is a good idea. Similarly, capturing such events in the internal newsletter also creates a public historical record. For example, the other day one of the authors of this book was in a local supermarket. He had stopped by to pick up a gallon of milk only to discover that the store had run out of the gallon size. He grabbed a half-gallon jug instead. At check-out the clerk asked him if he'd found everything he needed. When he told her that he come to buy a gallon of milk but they were out of the gallon size, she dashed to the back of the store, grabbed another half gallon, brought it up to the register, and gave it to him for free. He was impressed enough with this clerk's sense of service to tell all of us about the incident. This is the kind of story that belongs in the internal newsletter. It is an *Identity* story.

In Dunn, North Carolina, a local newspaper had somehow achieved an astounding local market penetration of 112% of households. How did they do it? The founder of the paper was

Hoover Adams. His strategy was simple: "Names, Names, and Names." In each issue of the paper he printed as many names of local people as possible. People love to see their name in print.

Hoover's idea is a good model for any internal company newsletter. It is all about getting as many employee names into the paper as you can. To the extent possible, any event that enhances an individual's desired *Identity* is fodder for a story. With the right focus, *Identity* is a powerful motivational tool.

Meaning

Meaning is how we derive personal *Meaning* from the work we do and the role we play. It encompasses accomplishment, self-creation, problem solving, the sense of mastery, and doing good. This can vary greatly across the employee population. Ultimately it is how each of us creates *Meaning* for ourselves. It can be expressed as: accomplishment, self-creation, problem solving, the sense of mastery, and doing good, or in other ways. Fundamentally we want to do *Meaning*ful work. How this is done varies by individual. Purpose matters.

Dr Sherry Moss Ph.D. is a professor at Wake Forest who writes about finding *Meaning* in work. One of her former students went to work for Walmart:

> "*I knew that Katharina had a bright future ahead of her, but wondered if she had chosen the right job. I mean, Walmart? So when I met her for dinner six months after she started her new job as an Associate Marketing Manager, I asked her all about her work. When I got to the important question, "Do you find Meaning in your work?" I was taken aback by her response. It went something like this:*"

> "*Before I started working at Walmart, I was asked which areas of the business I wanted to work in. My first choice was the grocery business because I consider myself a "foodie," but, more importantly, I try to incorporate as much fresh and healthy*"

food into my diet as possible. If there is one company that can change the way Americans eat, it's Walmart. And I knew before joining the company that I wanted to be a part of that."
"What I find the most meaningful about my job is the ability to work in an area that I am passionate about, and that is providing all Americans with access to healthier food. I'm fortunate to work for a company that is embracing this ideal and whose core customer is the everyday American."

A few months later Walmart announced a program to work with their suppliers to transition into selling healthier foods. (Moss n.d.)

When creating *Meaning* we begin with the premise that every job in the company is essential. If it were not essential, we wouldn't have someone doing that work. This includes everyone from the night watchman to the CEO.

Making *Meaning*

Making *Meaning* is tailored to each individual in their specific job. Ultimately you want to work with every individual to find *Meaning* in the work he or she does. The *Peer-to-Peer Accountability* group is responsible for helping each member of the peer group find *Meaning* through their work.

A good place to begin is to link the work done in their individual positions to the company's Core Ideology. Where possible you should translate the link to Core Ideology into *Meaning* for the individual. Begin the process by explaining the Core Purpose and Core Values of the company. If those things help you create your own *Meaning* in the company, you can explain how the company's Core Purpose and Core Values do that for you. You want the employee to start thinking about why the work is *Meaning*ful to them or how they might find *Meaning* in the work.

Some employees will find inspiration in the company's Core Ideology. Others will need to structure their own *Meaning* more organically. To further the conversation the peer group can use a list of intrinsic goods which is how people typically find *Meaning* in their work.

For Example:
- Making the world a better place (ask how?)
- An expression of self-creation
- Passion for a tangible outcome
- Creating status by doing important things for society
- A calling to help others
- Being a member of a team
- Work as a source of fun
- Complete belief in what the company does
- Provider for the family
- Fulfilling a sense of duty
- Solving difficult problems
- Creating a sense of accomplishment
- Winning
- Developing and teaching others
- Investing for the future
- Gaining Power
- Be a paradigm
- Creating independence/autonomy
- To work with others who matter to me

Use this as the basis for a discussion.[21]

Ultimately the peer group wants to structure <u>every</u> job such that it is very apparent to the person in the job why and how the work creates *Meaning* for them. To complete this process for every person and every job is work. For greater ease you might have your peer group do the following:

---

[21] This list is based on a list created by Sherri Moss PhD. You can see her full list with notes under the "sources of meaning" tab at: <u>www.meaningsource.org</u>.

Begin with the employee who seems to be the most motivated. (Whenever we tackle a new process, especially one involving personalities, we recommend finding and starting with the easiest case.) Work with this individual and build the link to *Meaning* by first inquiring, where they find real joy in their work, or what gives them the most satisfaction. You can give them a menu choice such as the one above.

Together, you want to find a way to build their source of joy into the job they have. Ask the employee to describe what they do in their own words. Next take the person through the 'five whys'. Ask why <u>what</u> they do is important. Then ask why <u>that</u> is important. Keep asking the next 'why' question until you get to an intrinsic good. If that intrinsic good does not match the one they selected for themselves before (they could have selected more than one), then point this out to them and ask them if it is this new reason that makes the work meaningful for them.

It is unlikely the answer will be 'no'. However, if the answer is 'no', then the job may not be the right fit for the employee, or perhaps the job is not good for any person. Sometimes a company does a poor job of structuring a job. If the job structure does not allow for making *Meaning*, then the job needs to be restructured. If the job is not essential to the core purpose of the business, then chances are the job should be eliminated.

Once you and your peers have articulated how the work can create *Meaning* for that person, you will want to revisit it time and again to reinforce it. A key responsibility for the peer group is to keep the employee focused on what makes the job meaningful to that employee. The more creatively this is done, the more often you can do it. The more often you do it, the better it is for you and your fellow employee.

Once you've drafted this for the easiest case, go to the next most motivated person. Do this until everyone in the peer group has established *Meaning*. Expect this will get modified over time.

If you end up with an employee for whom you cannot provide this, you must decide if it is the job or the person. If it is the job, then see if there is a better fit for the person elsewhere in the company. Otherwise, if it is the person, you should bring in senior leadership. They might have to give that employee the opportunity to find *Meaning* elsewhere.

Meaning for an employee can mature over time. Don't be afraid to let the *Meaning* for the employee change over time.

Accountability

Once an individual's *Identity* and *Meaning* have been defined they are added to the Colleague Letter of Commitments (see chapter on Structure) When everyone is working to sustain each individual's *Identity* and *Meaning* then you've create an environment where people feel they are contributing to a meaningful enterprise. When this occurs people naturally form close relationships. *Identity, Meaning* and valued relationships make it far less likely that someone will leave the company, especially if it would have been for a bump in salary.

Peer-to-Peer Accountability plays an important role in enhancing the company's ability to sustain *Identity* and *Meaning*. For *Peer-to-Peer Accountability* to work well you need to foster strong relationships. We will cover this fully in our chapter on *Peer-to-Peer Accountability*.

Leadership Behavior

Previously we pointed out that behavior is all you get from your employees. The same is true of leaders. Leadership behavior is behavior that is intended to influence the behaviors of others. When someone is in a leadership position, others employees may view that person's behavior as an example of how to behave. When you are a leader, everything you do can be seen as intentionally directed towards influencing others. Therefore, a good leader moderates his or her behavior with that caveat in mind.

We use a simple criterion to determine if a behavior is a worthy behavior. If you can answer, 'Yes' to this question, then it is worthy behavior: "Does this leadership behavior have a net positive impact on the employees' behavior <u>and</u> employees' motivation?" If it doesn't, or if you don't know what the impact will be, beware!

Learning Leadership
Far and away, the most bountiful source of Leadership beliefs and practices is experience. In that respect Leadership is a phenomenological art. The problem with experience is that it is remarkably unreliable. Unfortunately repetition has incredible

power to persuade us of the value of a behavior irrespective of the actual outcome.

When it comes to leadership behavior we are going to ask you to do something that is difficult. We want you to be open to questioning the validity of your existing leadership beliefs and practices.

In the second volume of this book we will discuss decision-making in and take a deep dive into the psychology behind making great decisions. Because we define leadership behavior before we discuss decision-making we want to introduce a small section of Decision Advantage™ (in volume two) here. This will be helpful since our typical leadership behavior is based more on phenomenological experience than on good analysis.

It is useful to have a tool to deal with this phenomenological experience before we let it influence our leadership behavior too greatly. Two areas of interest are relevant here. First, is to understand two aspects of how we learn: repetition and feedback. Second, we will teach a methodology for dealing with key assumptions.

First, let's look a basic example of how we can get things mixed up. It is an extreme example, however it represents how we learn certain behaviors and makes the fallacy clear.

Punishment works!

We have all heard that a carrot is better than a stick. Not everyone believes this. Some believe punishment works, praise doesn't. Here's proof. (You can do this experiment yourself.)

You have three marbles in an opaque bag. The marbles are identical except one marble is green, and two marbles are blue. You tell your employee that he will pull out two of the three without peeking into the bag. He must take out one marble at a time and show it to you. Using his sense of touch, his job is to remove only blue marbles. His behavior will be punished or rewarded after the first pull and his learning will be evident in the second pull. Punishment is a stiff reprimand. Praise is a friendly pat on the back. We will determine the effectiveness of this teaching technique based on that second pull.

You will discover that when you praise the first pull, subsequent pull only gets the right behavior about half the time. However, when you find yourself punishing the first pull, the second pull is the right behavior pretty consistently. Hence, punishment works far better than praise.

Obviously this is a joke. If his first pull is a blue marble he will be rewarded with a friendly pat on the back. What then remains in the bag are one blue marble and one green marble. His chance of pulling a blue marble is 50/50. Hence the second attempt will result in the green marble being selected about half the time.

However, if the first pull is a green marble then he will be reprimanded. What is left in the bag are two blue marbles. With this second pull he will exhibit the desired behavior every time by drawing out a blue marble. Hence, punishment works!

To imply there is something valid to learn from this exercise about the value of punishment or praise is a fallacy. The punishment or praise has no bearing on performance. The performance is determined based on statistics, or very simple math in this case. We wouldn't expect you to conclude that punishment works better than praise because the fallacy is obvious. However, when we make this a little more 'real world' the ability to see the fallacy gets cloudy as Daniel Kahneman discovered.

Long before he won the Nobel Prize, Kahneman ran into a similar situation when he was working with the Israeli Air Force.[22] He'd given a training talk in which he said that rewarding good performance worked better than punishing mistakes. One of the seasoned flight instructors in the room had a different point of view. The flight instructor went on to explain his beliefs using the example of a cadet learning aerobatic maneuvers. When the instructor praised a particularly well-executed maneuver, the very next time the cadet performed the maneuver; it was usually not as good. On the other hand when he found himself screaming into a cadet's headset for a badly executed maneuver, the next time it was performed better.

This is the same situation you run into whenever there is a statistically natural variation in performance, especially when we are learning something new. On average a person learning something will do it well one time and not as well the next. The better the performance the more likely the next one will not be quite as good. The same is true of bad performance; the likelihood is that the next one will be improved. The flight instructor was giving his feedback too much causal credit for what turns out to be a natural statistical phenomenon.

How we learn

Repetition and the immediacy of feedback impact what and how we learn. A good example of this is how we learn to drive a car.

When we are learning to drive the easiest thing to learn is how to steer. That is because you steer constantly and the feedback is immediate. Likewise the feedback in braking is immediate; however you brake less frequently and it takes a little longer to master. The common denominator between steering and breaking is that the behavior and the feedback happen in

---

[22] D. Kahneman, Thinking Fast and Slow, 2011, p.175. We use this book as a text book when we teach decision stewardship in Decision Advantage.

uninterrupted pairs? That is, the feedback follows immediately after the behavior. The closer these are to one another the more effective and accurate the learning can be.

When there is a lag between the behavior and the feedback, the feedback becomes less potent. For example, if you have the inclination to make Korean Kim Chi you will spend hours in preparing the cabbage and then have to wait at least three weeks for the taste feedback. In the intervening time you've had ample opportunity to forget some of the details of what you did and it may be hard for you to duplicate exactly what you did. Learning is impeded by this long gap between behavior and feedback.

The problem is further compounded when the behavior is repeated before receiving feedback for the first behavior. For example, take a young HR staffing person. As part of her job, she interviews five to six people every day. Weeks later, one out of those five or six may get hired. Whether or not that person turns out to be a good employee isn't clear for many weeks. In the meantime the staffing person has interviewed over a hundred other people. The feedback is too far removed from the actual interview process to provide a learning opportunity for the HR staffing person. However, that doesn't stop her from developing confidence in her interviewing ability.

When Daniel Kahneman was a young infantry officer assigned to the Israeli Army Psychology Branch he helped evaluate candidates for officer training. They used a technique of observing a team of leaderless candidates as they solved a problem. The problem was one they borrowed from the British Army. The task was to lift a log over a 6-foot high wall and get all the men over the wall without the log touching the ground or the wall, and without the candidates touching the wall either. It usually took many attempts and several different approaches. Kahneman and a colleague would observe and note how individuals in the group behaved. Based on these observations they would collaborate to create a coherent analysis of how each candidate would perform in officer training. They made these predictions with great confidence.

Every so often, they would receive feedback on how the candidates actually performed as cadets. When they compared their assessments with the actual cadet performance they discovered a consistent pattern: their ability to predict cadet performance was only slightly better than a blind guess. This was discouraging news. It showed that their evaluation process was fundamentally a waste of time.

Of course, it was the Army after all and the valueless nature of the enterprise did not dissuade the Army from continuing to use the technique. What's remarkable about this is that despite the feedback to the contrary, Kahneman and his colleagues maintained their confidence in their ongoing assessments. They knew that historically their assessments had added no value. Yet each time they did their observations and compiled their coherent stories on each candidate's potential, their knowledge of the past did not influence their process or, more remarkably, their absolute confidence in their current assessments. This time they were sure they got it right. However, they never did.

It turns out this behavior is normal. It is how our brains work. It suggests that the often repeated Einstein quote "Insanity: doing the same thing over and over again and expecting different results," isn't about insanity[23]. The behavior isn't insane, it's only irrational. Lots of our natural behaviors seem irrational[24].

---

[23] In business often the flipside of this definition is true. "Insanity: doing the same thing over and over again and expecting the same results." That's because in business: markets change; customer tastes change; the competition changes; or any number of other things interrupt the previous cause and effect relationship.

[24] See the terrific book by Daniel Ariely "Predictably Irrational"

Therefore, in cases where there are many intervening instances of the specific behavior before getting feedback on that behavior, the feedback becomes irrelevant, even if it is consistently negative. This is particularly true when the feedback is separated from the behavior by time and by additional instances of similar behavior, i.e. the feedback is long delayed and not consecutive.

For our HR staffing person we mentioned above, doing many interviews will convince her that she is becoming skilled at the task even if none of the people hired turn out to be as good as she'd predicted. The real feedback is too far removed from the interview, and many other intervening interviews blur the memory of the original behavior. Instead she will substitute other feedback, like how she feels after an interview; or how well she asked questions; or how well she listened; or how much she liked the candidate. These are things that give her instant feedback. Her brain will use this substitute feedback to build her confidence in the behavior. Subsequent feedback will not shake that confidence. Over time she will become very confident of her interviewing ability. You can approach almost anyone who is involved in interviewing and show them data that proves interviewing is largely a wasted effort. They will generally agree that the data is convincing. However, in their own minds they don't believe it applies to their individual ability. They *know* they are the exception. They are good at interviewing. This is a feeling we all share in one area of expertise or another.

Much of what we believe is true of leadership is learned in this way. And we don't question our own ability. If you are going to get the best out of your people you will need to be open to question your own behavior. It will also be useful to have a mechanism to validate your beliefs.

The mental processes that enable our HR staffing person and Daniel Kahneman and his colleagues to make judgments consists of a set of principles based on assumptions. We need a way to deal with assumptions that may or may not be causally linked to outcomes. In this circumstances it is useful to look at how others handle the problem, especially in institutions where their stakes are much higher than our own.

Key Assumptions Check

With the Afghan and Iraqi wars, the US Army has faced new more dangerous and more complex situations than in the past. The Key Assumptions Check is one of the new structured analytic techniques for dealing with complexity that the US Army borrowed from the CIA. It is part of what it calls the Army's Red Team methodology. The Army *"defines Red Teaming as a function to avoid groupthink, mirror imaging, cultural missteps, and tunnel vision in plans and operations. Red Teams help staffs avoid making poor assumptions and account for the complexity inherent in the Operational Environment."* (University of Foreign Military and Cultural Studies 2012, 1)

We are using the Key Assumption Check for a very specific reason. As a leader, you are not disposed to question the practices you hold as 'beyond question'. Those practices may turn out to be valid. However, your effectiveness in the behavioral leadership role depends upon your ability and willingness to examine even those things you hold dear. The Key Assumption Check calls for this type of examination.

The US Army uses a four-step process to perform the Key Assumption Check. Analysts, according to Army doctrine, depend upon certain premises whenever they are called upon to perform analysis. We all play the analysts' role when we think through decisions. We do not routinely call into question the premises upon which we make decisions. To help the analyst do a better job the following four steps are helpful[25]:

1. Review the current analytic line on the issue and write out the argument.
2. Articulate the necessary and sufficient premises that support the argument's validity.
3. Challenge each assumption as though you are the cross-examiner. How could you prove that a premise <u>must be</u> true? How could you show its opposite is false? Do the proofs.
4. Refine the argument including only the premises, which must be true. Is the original solution supported by this smaller set of premises? Could an alternate solution also be supported by this shortened list of premises?

Analytic Line

The first place where an argument may collapse is with the analytic line. The analytic line is the set of premises or steps that build the convincing argument. Have someone look at the steps you've articulated. A good analyst should be able to tell you if the line is valid: i.e. the conclusion follows from the premises. If it doesn't you may have to add or remove premises. Take the revised analytic line through steps 2-4.

True Premises

The hardest part of the Key Assumption Check is challenging the premises. It is very hard for you to challenge your own premises. Bias is insidious. Every decision we make is influenced by our individual biases. The problem with biases is that we are unaware of them in ourselves. We all live under the illusion that we can put aside our biases and make a well

---

[25] We have a couple of fun exercises we use to teach this technique. We are happy to share one of these with anyone desiring to employ this methodology in their business. Send us a request via Info@thnk2grow.com.

thought-out, unbiased evaluation of something. However, as a recent Harvard Business Review article pointed out: executives cannot do much about their own biases. The best we can hope for is to rely on our ability to recognize a bias in others and figure out how to remove its influence. (Lovallo, Sibony and Kahneman 2011)

In the Key Assumption Check, the two important questions to ask of any premise are 1) How can I prove the premise? 2) How can I disprove the premise? An unacceptable answer to these questions is, "I cannot prove or disprove the premise, nevertheless, I know it is true." The consequence of this answer is that you must remove the premise from the analytic line, which will likely undermine the validity of the argument. It is a strict discipline; if you can't articulate a way to prove the truth of the premise then the premise is not allowed.

Key Assumption Check

Leadership Behavior	Impact on Employee Behavior	Assumptions in the Analytic Line	How to prove	Proven
				☐ Yes ☐ No
	Impact on Employee Motivation	Assumptions in the Analytic Line	How to prove	Proven
				☐ Yes ☐ No

As a leader the most effective way to deal with this issue is to avoid being the one to present the analytic line in the first place. It is easier to challenge someone else's line than it is to challenge your own, even if their line supports the conclusion you have already drawn. In doing this exercise you ask yourself ,"What do we know, and what don't we know?" For assertions where we think we know something, probe for the source of the confirming information. Whenever people play a role of the source, you must examine what their motivation might be as well as the quality of the evidence they produce. Keep in mind that experience is not always as valid as people believe it is. If it is a technical source, beware of poorly produced technical conclusions.

In the remainder of this chapter you will take your best shot at defining leadership behavior. You will come back later to refine it. For now getting it about 80% right is very good work, and a basic Key Assumption Check will get you there.

Remember when delving into the process of defining leadership behaviors for your company, you will have to work hard to keep an open mind. The leadership behaviors you will choose are purposeful behaviors with two objectives.

First, leadership behaviors must support getting the desired behaviors from your employees. This was covered in the first chapter of this book.

Second, leadership behaviors must ensure that the motivators we talked about in the last chapter are supported. Many managers behave in ways that get the employee behavior they want in the short run, while undermining motivators in the long run. It is easy to do. For example, the manager behaves uncivilly while instructing an employee to get something done. As reported in the Harvard Business Review, 98% (of thousands of employees surveyed) said they'd experienced uncivil behavior in the workplace. Half of those surveyed said they experience that behavior every week. Nearly everyone who experiences such behavior at work responds in a negative way. They will work shorter hours; decrease their effort; decrease the quality of their work; waste time worrying about the manager's behavior; avoid interacting with the offender; lose a sense of commitment to the organization and its purpose; cease to be as creative; lose team spirit; and perhaps worst of all, take their frustration out on customers. (Porath and Pearson 2013)

Motivators and behaviors are prime assets of the company. They are company property. They do not belong to managers. Your managers are stewards of these assets. Doing anything that undermines these assets will reduce the value of the company. What CEO wants to pay for this type of behavior.

Leadership behavior

Perhaps the best leadership advice ever given was advice Dr. Robert Sutton gave to a CEO. He advised, "Hire a bunch of smart people, and stay out of their way until they ask for your help." When defining leadership behavior be stingy. Less is more.

You will notice, since the chapter is about to end, that we are not prescribing any specific leadership behavior here. Your situation and your company is unique. You should strive to be rigorous in ensuring that whatever leadership behaviors you put on the Behavioral Grid answers this question with a 'Yes': "*Does this leadership behavior have a net positive impact on both employee behavior and employee motivation?*"

Where to start? When it comes to defining leadership behaviors the easiest place to begin is with deciding what leadership behaviors should be banned. These are behaviors which undermine either employee behavior, or employee motivation, or both. Don't be alarmed if initially the only behaviors you can honestly put on the form are banned behaviors.

The specific leadership behaviors you will choose will depend upon how you have defined your employee behavior and how you've broadly defined the motivational structure to enhance that behavior. Some fundamentals to keep in mind are:

Lead by example: Always walk the talk.

Be open and honest

Do not allow office politics to take hold
Be fair to the extreme.
Be available, not overbearing.
Support risk taking.

Accountability

Peer-to-Peer Accountability

There is some confusion around what *Peer-to-Peer Accountability* means. It has been described as "...when members support each other in getting the work of the team done." (Frohman n.d.) While this is true, it can be understood in a way that undermines genuine *Peer-to-Peer Accountability*.

The problem with the description above is the phrase "the work of the team". This can imply that the work is assigned to the team as a whole. Certainly some teams are given assignments like this. However, accountability works best in situations where a specific individual has sole responsible for a specific behavior. *Peer-to-Peer Accountability* means that this individual is responsible to the peer group for that specific behavior, and the peer group has the audit responsibility to keep that individual on tract to deliver the prescribed behavior. Back in the chapter on behavior we introduced the notion of accountability to include both these pieces: the individual is liable and answerable for his or her own behavior; and the group provides the audit function to ensure the right behavior emerges and the wrong behavior does not.

The discipline works well when each individual owns specific behaviors. The only thing the team has a shared responsibility for is this role of accountability. In the coming section on Structure, we will introduce the Three Questions. The team will also be accountable as a group for obtaining a score of 9 or 10 from everyone on the team answering the Three Questions. It's the primary goal of *Peer-to-Peer Accountability* .

Getting Teamwork

Teamwork happens only when individuals on the team behave in the appropriate fashion. They are accountable for their behavior as individuals. Whenever a 'to-do' is created, it is a crystal clear assignment of deliverables. This means you don't behave in a way where Johnny, Suzy, Fred, and Ella get together and decide they should create a marketing plan without defining who does what. The discipline means you must spend the time up front to define exactly what Johnny is going to deliver and what Suzy is going to deliver, etc. Every assignment must meet the SMART criteria. (Specific, Measurable, Actionable, Results focused, and Time-bound.) We love simple solutions and this idea of specific accountability is very simple.

Implementing Behavioral Advantage™ is easier if you already have an operating methodology in-place. The operating methodology inculcates both the audit discipline and individual behavioral responsibility into running the business. If a business does not have such an operating methodology in place we strongly recommend the Entrepreneurial Operating System (EOS)[26]. One of the key benefits of the EOS methodology is that it installs the foundation of *Peer-to-Peer Accountability* quite

---

[26] We implement EOS and can recommend other implementers around North America.

subtly. Otherwise, when we implement Behavioral Advantage™ you will first establish the *Peer-to-Peer Accountability* foundation.

When it comes to behavior, *Peer-to-Peer Accountability* is profoundly powerful. However, for *Peer-to-Peer Accountability* to work the foundational elements of trust and cooperation need to permeate the peer group. Charles Darwin first suggested the idea that groups function best when trust and cooperation are the group's foundation.

Sometimes when people talk about trust in the workplace they focus on hierarchical trust: trust between boss and subordinate. *"Yet the problem is not that you don't trust your boss, but that he doesn't trust you, or anyone working for him, for that matter."* (Guthrie 2012) While trust in that relationship is important, more important to business outcomes is trust among peers.

Trust requires an open and honest dialogue. When we begin working with companies our first order of business it to get the team members to trust one another and cooperate. Trust takes time. We accelerate trust-building to the extent possible through the use of dialogue based exercises. The best indicator that trust has been established on a team is that team members can discuss an issue where there is conflict and the conflict never gets personal. Only when trust is firmly in place do we start the work on behaviors and motivators. However, we never stop working on, and building trust.

To create the necessary level of caring about one another you can employ various team building exercises. We ask you to employ a simple method that has consistently worked well in over 500 companies across many industries for the past 10 years. At the beginning of every meeting we do a 'Check-in'. This serves to separate the meeting from the rest of the work day, and it gives each of you a chance to get to know one another better. The Check-in is a quick one minute update. You go around the table as each person shares a piece of personal good news and a piece of business good news. The manager must set this up properly. You want the personal good news to be personal. Otherwise, you'll get superficial stories, perhaps about a golf game someone played over the weekend. The manager sets the bar by sharing something truly personal, e.g. "My wife and I have been sweating over our daughter admission into graduate school. We were concerned that when she came home for Thanksgiving she'd be crabby if she was still waiting to hear. Fortunately, the day before she was to come home she got a phone call notifying her she'd been accepted into her first-choice school! Thanksgiving was terrific as a result."

Another way to help a team come together is to use something called a "prosocial incentive/reward mechanism". For example: you reward the team after their third week of implementing Behavioral Advantage™ . Each member of the peer group gets $50. However, they don't get to spend the money on themselves. Instead, on a random selection basis each must spend the $50 on a different member of the team. Allow them to be creative and the gift exchange should always be face-to-face.

The research on this form of incentive pay is fascinating. It turns out we get much more from the act of giving than we do from spending on ourselves. (Aknin, et al. 2010). Moreover, the firm is better off with this form of incentive. If you gave each member of the peer group $50 to spend on themselves, the firm can expect to get back only $15 of that (a net loss). However, in the prosocial model, where each person spends the $50 incentive on a teammate, then the firm gets back over $250. Plus, it pulls the team closer together. (Norton, et al. 2012, 9) It will take anywhere from four to eight weekly meetings to build sufficient trust to enable *Peer-to-Peer Accountability* . (see the chapter on Structure)

When we implement Behavioral Advantage we use the first four weeks of trust building to focus on something critical, but less sensitive to trust. We get the team really good at execution. The team must be able to get stuff done before you can effectively focus on behavior and motivation. We do a day of training, putting into place a set of tried and true tools that enable the team to get stuff done. Then we go away for four weeks.

When we come back, we do another day of training and in that day we define behaviors. Again we go away for four weeks as the trust building continues and when we come back the team is cohesive and ready to dive into and define individual motivation. At that point the training is complete. We then go into a quarterly cycle. During the first or second quarterly meeting we will introduce in the last critical tool. It enables empowerment and we will discuss it in the chapter on Structure.

To enable the team to go from a hierarchical top-down management to *Peer-to-Peer Accountability* it needs a structure of discipline. We use two simple tools to inculcate this structure of discipline. One is the Rated 10 Meeting which we will discuss in the chapter on Structure. The other is a simple document representing the 'contract' each member of the team sets up with peers. We call this contract the *Colleague Letter of Commitments*. It comprises the following elements:

Colleague Letter of Commitments
Personal Mission in the Business
List of the Behaviors I Agree to Produce
Scoreboard Item for Which I am Accountable (Weekly)
The Time I Will Commit to Accomplishing my Activities
My Identity – How I Wish Others to See Me
My Meaning – The Meaning I Strive to Get from the Work
My Current 90 Day Extra Goals
Colleague Sign-offs (All Members of the Peer Group)

We will note, as we come to them, what items go into *The Colleague Letter of Commitments.* When other members of the team sign off on your letter, they are agreeing that the defined behaviors, the scoreboard items, your time commitment, and your 90 day extra goals are all the right deliverables. In addition they agree that your personal mission statement, your *Identity* and your *Meaning* are all things they promise to support actively.

The *Colleague Letter of Commitments* may be modified at any point and is certainly modified at each quarterly meeting as new 90 day extra goals are established. Each time it is modified the team will sign the document.

Once the foundation of *trust* is in place, you will begin to define the behaviors required for each person in the peer group based on their role in the company. Earlier we talked about the leadership team defining company-wide behaviors in support of how you treat customers, how you differentiate yourselves with customers, and how you create competitive advantage. Now the peer group will apply these to individual positions. The peer group's job is to define these behaviors such that they work well for the position at hand. It is not a requirement that these behaviors match the broad behaviors defined by the leadership team. For example, a credit card company might define certain behaviors for its customer service representatives. These behaviors would likely be quite different from the behaviors defined for their bad-debt collectors.

Defining behaviors will have no value unless people actually behave in the prescribed way and avoid behaving in any of the banned ways. Accountability is the key to ensuring you get the right behaviors. The power of *Peer-to-Peer Accountability* is extraordinary and we will place much of this work on the shoulders of the peer group. It is in the peer group that we will define individual behaviors and motivators. It is within and through the peer group that you will work to get and keep 100% of your people fully engaged.

When accountability is a discipline, work gets done. In the chapter on Structure we will talk about the weekly Rated 10 meeting and the 90 Day Goal Setting meeting. We use both meetings to create the discipline of accountability. If you rely solely on the boss to be the agent of that accountability then you are not maximizing the power of the discipline. *Peer-to-Peer Accountability* carries a social value missing from the boss to subordinate relationship. Most businesses today do not employ *Peer-to-Peer Accountability* . Most businesses rely on the boss to hold subordinates accountable. This is what Patrick Lencioni calls a practice of an unhealthy organization. It undermines your ability to get the most out of your people.

Setting Behavior

Peer-to-Peer Accountability starts with individual buy-in. The first step is to ensure that the individual fully grasps what behavior he or she is expected to deliver. The individual should embrace the behavior, and fully comprehend the reason behind the behavior.

> *In the introduction of this book we talked about a study that showed better financial results correlated with self-managed behaviors. In California the notion of Peer-to-Peer Accountability has been taken to the extreme of self-managed behaviors. Morning Star Company is a very successful business that has built its entire management structure around Peer-to-Peer Accountability. What does that management structure look like? Well, there are no managers. There are no bosses. "No one has a boss, employees negotiate responsibilities with their peers, everyone can spend the company's money, and each individual is responsible for procuring the tools needed to do his or her work." We do not go that far here, and you can read*

more about Morning Star Company in the Big Idea section of the December 2011 Harvard Business Review.[27]

Every employee must be able to see how their role fits into the company's Vision. They also must be able to see how their work aligns to their personal sense of mission. These two ideas form the basis for the employee's Personal Mission statement which lays out how he or she will contribute to the company's mission and goals in their own way. It should read like a true mission statement focused on some intrinsically good outcome valuable to the individual. The Personal Mission statement becomes the first entry in the *Colleague Letter of Commitments.*

The best place to begin working on behaviors is with the broad company objectives. In the chapter on Structure we talk about setting annual and quarterly goals. These form the foundation for how you begin to define goals and supporting behaviors for individual positions.

Every 90 days the company will translate its annual goal into a 90 Day Mission statement and 90 day goals for the company. These trickle down to each peer group and form the <u>special</u> 90-day extra goals for each individual on the team. These goals are separate from the day to day routine work for the individual. They are the big things that need to change to move the business forward. Keep these to a small number, you want a very high completion rate.

We group these goals into 90 day increments because this has been shown to be the length of time people can remain well focused. If you allow for more time, then people may become

---

[27] Other companies have built organizational structures similar to Morning Star. For example, Semco in Brazil, W. L. Gore & Associates, Valve Corporation, and others.

sidetracked before completing the objectives. 90 days is a short enough period to keep everyone in the company rowing in the same direction. This discipline requires structure, which we cover in the chapter on Structure. The next step is to take the list of the current 90-Day Goals for this individual (there should be no more than five) and add these to the *Colleague Letter of Commitments*. (In the Structure chapter we talk briefly about creating these 90-day deliverables.)

When you begin to define behaviors you begin with the individual's Personal Mission statement and the requirements of his or her role in the company. For this process, every member of the *Peer-to-Peer Accountability* group should be in the room. This team consists of the employee, his or her manager, and his or her peers in the department. For this behavior definition process you may also include people who interact with the individual across departments.

The first time you do this, you will go through a behavior definition process as a group. Each person in the peer group individually makes a list of the key behaviors required for each deliverable (routine work and 90 Day Goals). Then, these are captured on the white board. You put this list through the "Purge, Pair, or Preserve" process. Then, using this bigger list, each individual selects five behaviors for each deliverable and scores them "5" for the most important, "4" for next, and so on. The scored for each behavior are summed and the top five (more or less) are entered into the grid for this position. This same process is followed to get the banned behaviors.

With each step, the employee, whose position is being defined, must agree with the selected behaviors. If the employee disagrees at any point, then their reasons for disagreeing must be carefully evaluated. Often people who are in a particular position see its nuance more perspicuously than outsiders do. Their arguments should be listened to and given extra weight.

Significant leeway should be granted to the employee to define the position's behaviors. It is human nature to want to do things the way you think they should be done. If you are forced to do things in a different way, you may execute those behaviors without the expectancy of success. By itself, this can remove the opportunity for success. The advice here is sometimes people are right about their own behavior. If their perspective differs from the group, then giving them the chance to show they are right -- or learn they are wrong -- is a good investment. Make it clear that in the next few weeks the behavior either gets the desired results or the individual will utilize the behavior suggested by the peer group.

If the group believes it is a good idea you may include banned behaviors as well.

However, no behavior should be allowed that either undermines someone else's behavior, or undermines the motivational structure of the position.

The behaviors then get added to the *Colleague Letter of Commitments*. (When you first do this you will realize that it's better to have a short powerful behaviors' list than a long, broad list.)

Individual *Identity* and *Meaning*

Getting the right behaviors is the first step. To get the most value from the individual, these behaviors need to be highly motivated behaviors.

Identity is the first component of our motivational model. The employee must be able to establish a desired *Identity* through the work done in this position. You begin by allowing everyone in the room to individually and privately write down the key elements of *Identity*, which this position seems likely to provide. You look for things like expertise, authority, status, service, etc.

Then the employee in question lets the group know what he or she has defined as the key components of *Identity* and how he or she wishes to be seen in the company. The peer group members will contribute their own ideas around *Identity* for the position. The employee in question has the final word. Once the nature of the desired *Identity* is established then the group determines how they can contribute to creating and maintaining the *Identity* the employee has chosen. This will be refined over time through the periodic attention the individual receives from the peer group in the weekly Rated 10 Meeting (see below).

The *Identity* for this person is added to the *Colleague Letter of Commitments*. When the peer group sights off on the letter they are committing themselves to support the individual to realize this *Identity* (and *Meaning*).

Next we tackle *Meaning*. Similarly, as we did with *Identity*, we want each member of the peer group to independently capture what they think creates *Meaning* for this position. These are thing like problem solving, a sense of mastery, doing some good, self-creation, etc. Again the employee identifies what *Meaning* he or she sees in the work and the team contributes ideas to enhance that *Meaning*. The *Meaning* for this person is added to the *Colleague Letter of Commitments*.

It is possible that during the process the individual in question recognizes that this is not a good fit for him or her. In that case an effort should be made to see if there is a position that better matches the capabilities and motivations for this person. However, if no such position is available, then you must let the individual find success elsewhere. Sooner or later we all run into people who are working for the wrong company, or are in the wrong position. The Behavioral Advantage™ methodology is perhaps the most open way to enable very different people to work together.

The final step is a daily log of behaviors. In the beginning the employee should keep a daily log of behaviors. As part of the trial period (60-90 days) they should write down, at the end of the day, examples of the required behaviors they engaged in during that day. Likewise, if they engaged in banned behaviors those examples should also be captured. A tool like the web based *I done this* https://idonethis.com can serve as a tracking and accountability tool.

Likewise, the individual should also log how he or she was able to experience the *Identity* and *Meaning* of the position. The purpose is to keep the behaviors and motivators fresh for the individual. It is more likely people will engage in the right behaviors if those behaviors become habits.

Individual Accountability

Although it may not be necessary to repeat this, when we talk about *Peer-to-Peer Accountability* we don't remove any element of self-accountability. You are 100% responsible for your own behavior. Being provoked provides no excuse. You are 100% accountable for what you say and do, and how you say it and how you do it.

Behavior & Motivation in the Weekly Meetings

In addition to building relationships in the weekly meeting, we want to accomplish something extraordinarily useful for the business in these meetings. The peer group plays the primary role in keeping people in line with behavior and the two motivators, *Identity* and *Meaning*.

You will see the in the weekly Rated 10 Meeting agenda that it contains an item called "Team Member Focus (see the weekly meeting agenda in the chapter on Structure.) On a rotational basis each week, one person defends their *Colleague Letter of Commitment.* They are the subject of the team's evaluation, input, and support. The person in question fills out the Behavioral Check-list for himself or herself. Additionally the person will self-assess their success in creating and maintaining the desired *Identity,* and finding good *Meaning* in the work.

Prior to the weekly meeting each member of the peer group will also independently fill out the Behavioral Checklist for this person, including their success around creating *Identity* and *Meaning.*

The group will discuss any gaps the person identified for himself or herself, and any different perspectives from the peer group. The purpose of this effort is to ensure that the person is on track with the right behaviors, and is able to create the desired *Identity* and *Meaning* and is getting the right stuff done. It is the peer group's mandate to work together to find the best pathway to success for this individual. In other words the idea is to be helpful, not critical and not patronizing. The last thing to do as part of Team Member Focus is you ask the person the Three Questions. The goal is to get a '9' or '10' for each of the Three Questions:

1. *"On a scale of 1 to 10, how likely is it that you would recommend our company as a place of employment to a qualified friend or relative?"*
2. *"On a scale of 1 to 10, how successful are you at creating the Identity you have set out for yourself from the work you do?"*
3. *"On a scale of 1 to 10, how successful are you at creating the Meaning you want from the work you do?"*

The peer group is responsible to getting everyone on the team up to a '9' or '10'. This must be genuine. You can't just say you've achieved that level, you must actually achieve that level of success. The peer group must agree that you've genuinely achieved a '9' or '10'. Ultimately the peer group must be convinced. The peer group is accountable for this result from every member of the group. It and has the authority to tackle issues that get in the way, including bad bosses.

TEAM MEMBER NAME	JOAN	FRED	JANE	FAROUK	Average	Benchmark
DESIRED BEHAVIORS						
Keep promises to customers regaring resolving customer enquiries, and complaints before the date and time promised to the customer	+	+	+	+-	+	+
Refrain from saying "I think". Instead when dealing with internal customers ask a question starting with "How do we"	+-	+-	+	+	+-	+-
With customers and colleagues, listen first, then listen again.	+	-	+	+	+	+
Always bring 'A' game. Be disciplined, organized, and accountable. Help peers behave well.	+-	+	+	+	+	+
BANNED BEHAVIORS						
Talkin about colleagues behind their backs.	-	+-	-	-	-	+-
Lying to, being rude to, or misleading customers	-	-	-	-	-	-

In the Quarterly Goal Setting meeting the three questions must be answered by each individual on the team. This is part of evaluating how well the team did during the quarter. By the time an individual gets to their third Quarterly Goal Setting meeting he or she is expected to have achieved a '9' or '10' on all three of the questions. If not, that person may be in the wrong job, or may be wrong for the company. This should be handled as a 90-day Concern and go on the *CIPIO List*. (Pronounced Sipēō, it stands for Concerns, Issues, Problems, Ideas, Opportunities. See the chapter on Structure.)

The Role of *Peer-to-Peer Accountability*
Accountability only works if a specific individual is accountable for the action and results. In our case, the action is primary; the result is secondary. We don't want to overplay this card,

however, <u>always</u> we first want to focus on the behavior that produces the result. If you look only at the result, you may miss the critical cause, the behavior.

Peer-to-Peer Accountability means that an employee is not only responsible to the boss for his/her behavior. In fact, the employee is primarily responsible to their peer group (which in its broadest sense is everyone in the company). Thus, each employee's behavior is crucial to the success of the whole enterprise. It matters to everyone.

As a member of the peer group, your role is to help your peers deliver the behaviors for which they are accountable.

The weekly meeting is one vehicle for this; it's an ongoing responsibility. When an individual gets significantly out-of-line, then don't wait until the weekly meeting. As members of the peer group, your job is to step in and help that person get back into line. This takes a bit of finesse on everyone's part. The problem is the behavior, not the person. Treat it as such. Be delicate in identifying the concern.

If you are the person on the receiving end of the concern, your job is to be more analytic than defensive. If the concern is legitimate, then the dialogue is not about what happened in the past, but how to redress the concern going forward. If the concern is not legitimate then identify it as a difference of opinion, and get others engaged in the conversation right away. Resolve disputes quickly.

If the dispute persists, the last word belongs to the manager of the person whose behavior is in question. This is only after others have been brought into the conversation. In a company where *Peer-to-Peer Accountability* works well, this will be a very rare event.

Finally, when it comes to concerns around behavior, the boss always plays the role of leader, not manager. As leader, you must follow the behavioral precepts set out for the leaders in your organization.

Context

Context is about trying to help prevent the 'senior commanders from losing the battle'.

The gap in most leadership solutions is found in the connection between the things you do as leader and their long-term impact on motivation. It is such a big gap that it is hard to miss. Even Jim Collins, who wrote *Good to Great*, recognized this gap. In 2000 he wrote an article entitled "Aligning Action and Values" (J. Collins 2000). While he never gives up on the idea of values being guiding principles for behavior he tacitly admits they don't do the job. He concludes that what matters is active management around behaviors.

In the article, Collins talks about 3M, "3M, for instance, has always had a sense of its core values—sponsoring innovation, protecting the creative individual, solving problems in a way that makes people's lives better."

We already know that values are not what guide behavior. In fact, this whole idea of values driving behavior was not what was going on at 3M. Collins himself tells us this in the same article when he admits, "I don't even know if 3M has a formal "values statement" (if it does, we never came across it in all of our research into 3M)." The '3M values' he lists are <u>his</u> interpretation and classification of employee behavior. Collins goes on to say "…what really set 3M apart was the ability of its leadership over the years to create mechanisms that bring these principles to life and translate them into action." This is all about finding ways to drive behavior.

What makes this a useful article is Jim Collins' focus on this problem of alignment. You can throw out the whole discussion around values and the substance of his article remains. He points out that the key leadership activity is to recognize when misalignments exist and fix them.

Collins uses an example of a company that recognizes it is important to give people autonomy, and empower them to take action. One day the company has an issue. It implements a new service without getting all the required departments involved. As a result their customers are negatively impacted. It's a problem. In response a manager implements a set of ad hoc policies to ensure all possible stakeholders sign-off on future changes. In the moment it seemed like a reasonable way to prevent the problem. Over time this policy becomes a roadblock. Ultimately the ad hoc policies undermined the sense of autonomy and empowerment in the company. This was misalignment.

The word we use is "context". Our intention is not to introduce a new term, but to introduce a concept that includes the distinction between <u>aligning leadership behavior with employee behavior</u>, and <u>aligning leadership behavior with employee motivation</u>. These are two different things. Each warrants close attention. Leadership affects both employee behavior and employee motivation. And what we ask employees to do can impact their ability to tap into their motivators. Context is about explicitly recognizing these impacts and making sure your leadership team stays aligned on both.

When Context gets out of alignment, then who should fix it?

Look Inward, Angel

We take a very strong view: All problems in the business are leadership problems. This is the 100/0 concept as it is applied to business leadership. The 100/0 Leadership Principle says that you take full responsibility (the 100) for something, expecting nothing (the 0) of the other party. (Ritter 2010)

The behavior that the business obtains is the responsibility of leadership, 100% of the time. The responsibility of anyone else is 0%. Anytime things get out-of-whack the leadership team should look first at itself to ascertain if it is a leadership problem.

A couple of years ago I saw an industry survey that showed the majority of managers reported that what hinders innovation is the lack of good ideas from employees. The same survey showed that the majority of employees felt the biggest obstacle to innovation was management's illiberal mindset. The employees complained that managers shot-down every idea they came up with. We would be inclined to lean toward the employees' perspective, and history suggests that is correct.[28]

However, the 100/0 leadership principle is an empowering perspective. It says that as a leader you have the power to effect the change you want.

---

[28] In a prior book (Advantage) I talk about this issue and the data is pretty clear that the employees are right, manager mindsets get in the way more often than not.

Leadership must look inward first. Chances are the problem is in leadership behavior. One of our clients was struggling with their operations manager who was a terrific employee but when it came to the executive functions, he was out of his depth. For months we advised the CEO to face the hard conversation and resolving the issue. Initially he was very calm and composed when talking about the issue. We warned him that the longer he delayed, the more likely he would begin to get angry at his employee. This is exactly what happened. When the leadership team finally addressed the issue the CEO displayed his anger and frustration and his team turned it back around on him.

Everyone on the leadership team knew the operations manager was in over his head including the operations manager himself. They couldn't get the CEO to tackle the problem. The team ended up resolving the matter quite simply. Though the operations manager was great at some parts of his job; he wasn't inclined to the executive duties that went along with the position. They resolved to allow him to continue doing the parts of the job he loved and to hire someone to take on the executive duties. It might have turned out differently if the CEO had let the issue fester until he became so angry he fired the otherwise very valuable employee.[29]

The point is, it's the CEO whose behavior matters most. Next in line is the executive leadership team. Their behavior cascades down through the management ranks of the company.

Context links the behaviors of leaders to both the behaviors and motivators of workers. In the chapter on leadership we talked about utilizing leadership behaviors that support the employees in delivering the desired employee behaviors. As a leader, you

---

[29] This team was using the methods built into the Entrepreneurial Operating System. We facilitated the implementation of the system into this business and it engenders the open/honest dialogue that allowed them to come to a good solution.

want to define your behaviors such that they support the motivators as well.

The Key Assumption Check form that we gave you in the Leadership chapter can help. It is useful to review the check for every leadership behavior from time to time. Certainly, if you run into behavioral or motivational problems you want to first look at leadership, and this form can be helpful is sorting out why things are not working as expected.

Misalignments happen. For example, if among your core values you state something like, "We treat our employees, customers, and community with integrity and care." And, if over time internal pressure builds on your employees to bill your clients unethically (recall Jonah and the economics consulting firm) then this billing practice will begin to undermine all behaviors around integrity. Since the work is still getting done it is hard to see how this impacts the business. However, many studies have shown that motivated behavior tends to be far more productive. According to the Gallup Q12 study the two most meaningful measures around motivation are productivity and quality. In the study, Gallup reports an 18% lift in productivity and a whopping 60% lift in quality across entire companies where most employees are motivated. (Harter, et al. 2009) When this is broken down into individual teams the data is far more impressive. Gallup reports that where a team consists entirely of motivated people, the performance lift is a 240% boost in financial performance. (Van Allen 2009)

Raising the motivation of <u>some</u> employees, or even <u>most</u> employees is a timid goal. You end up wasting much of that incremental 240% financial lift. By utilizing Behavioral Advantage™ you will lift the entire workforce to being fully motivated. You wouldn't want to waste any of that 240%; particularly due to poorly thought through leadership behavior.

The task of evaluating a leadership behavior in terms of its impact on employee behavior and motivation takes commitment and diligence. The study of psychology is different from physics or chemistry where mathematical models and 'laws' can be more directly tested and applied. In cognitive science we are often only able to see the effect, not the cause. It is a little like trying to understand the character of the sun when all you can observe is a shadow. In cognitive science we leave lots of room for the exception. We like a psychological study in which 100% of the participants behave in the same way. That rarely happens. Think back to the Milgram experiments we talked about in the introduction. In that experiment, 100% of the participants pressed the button to administer every shock through the 300 volt level. However, if our hypothesis had been that everyone would follow orders right through to the maximum level of 450 volts, then we would have explain why a minority of participants did not behave that way.

The point is, be careful not to overreact to the exception. When you are evaluating the impact of a leadership behavior, step back and analyze the exceptions. They may be circumstances you will have to live with. The best check on the effectiveness of a leadership behavior is to ask the employees who are impacted by it. In Behavioral Advantage™ it is more likely the employees will alert you of the problem first.

Because your behaviors can change subtly before you notice the change, you will routinely police your leadership behavior for context. Ensure that a psychologically compatible environment exists between behaviors and the tenets of motivation. This is a leadership responsibility. When you implement Behavioral Advantage™ , your workers will likely let you know quickly and loudly when leadership behavior gets out of alignment.

In the next chapter we will talk about Structure. If the Structure you put into place works, then you should never have an issue with Context. If Context is an issue, then it is a behavioral problem in leadership.

Stucture

Structure ensures that the desired behaviors obtain, and the banned behaviors don't.

Structure as Policy

It is easy to fall into the trap of seeing the process of defining behaviors as draconian. It is not. Earlier we mentioned Method Cleaning Products. When Method grew beyond 'small company' status it faced the need to put structure in place. It struggled to balance the need for more structured process with the desire to preserve the culture they loved. They created behavioral guidelines designed to "channel the frenetic atmosphere of innovation and quixotic spontaneity so vital to our success." They stuck with the "values" nomenclature for these behavioral guidelines. The first is, "Keep Method Weird!" They want their people to feel some freedom to be exuberant. Other behavioral values included "Collaborate Like Crazy", "What Would MacGyver Do?", and "Innovate, Don't Imitate." (Ryan and Lowry 2011) These are not draconian guides. You want structure to enable the right behaviors. You do not want to stifle your people. When it comes to policy, a great rule of thumb is 'Less is More'.

Whatever behavioral guidelines you subscribe to, both in terms of desired behaviors and banned behaviors, there will be times when the better angels of our nature fail us. We are emotional beings and prone to letting our emotions get the better of us.

Jonathan Haidt's has a clever metaphor for human decision-making. It is the Elephant and the Rider. (Haidt 2006) The Rider is the thinking side: the part of our brains that can plan and think farther ahead. The Elephant is that more automatic side the part of our brains that is guided by wants, needs, and performs our unconscious actions. You can imagine in the metaphor when the Elephant and Rider are in conflict, the Elephant tends to get its way. For example, it is the Rider who decides to lose a little weight, and it's the Elephant that eats the late-night bowl of ice cream. It is also the Elephant who decides whom we like and whom we don't.

We are emotional creatures. The notion of establishing behaviors is not to create an army of robots. Rather behaviors are defined as desired behaviors and banned behaviors. And here, we are appealing to the 'Rider'. The purpose of any behavioral guide is to ensure that employees are acting in ways that best serve the goals of the enterprise. Fundamentally, the business pays for the behavior, whatever kind it is, because that is all the employee can deliver. It pays for good behavior, neutral, non-productive behavior, and bad behavior. The company has the expectation that it is paying for good productive behavior.

Company policy is created to preserve and protect the culture of behavior and motivation. It works very simply. Once behaviors are established and published, then any person in the company who observes another member of the company exhibiting a banned behavior may point out that behavior to the offender. It is the offender's immediate responsibility to say "You are right, I stand corrected." This is full-blown *Peer-to-Peer Accountability* . When it comes to banned behaviors, everyone is a peer!

The CEO is the Chief Structural Officer and is the most open recipient of behavioral coaching. The truth is we are all human, we get emotional. When this happens the elephant overrides the Rider and we say and do things that are driven by that emotional excitement.

This is often when the wrong behavior emerges. The proper moment to correct that behavior is the instant the emotion drains. The key insight is to give the offender, even the CEO, a moment to self-correct. Anytime an employee observes another employee exhibiting bad behavior, first, allow the offender a chance to self-correct. That means, waiting until the emotion behind the bad behavior dissipates. In situations where the offending employee fails to self-correct, then the observer must address the behavior. Perhaps saying, "I felt uncomfortable with what you did."

Some people are inclined to game the system. Here is an example: The company has a policy against behavior that personalizes people's input. Simply put the behavior policy states "We discuss the merits of the idea, not the attributes of the idea's originator or proponent."

Roy is an employee who routinely says things like: "With all love and kindness, your idea reveals a shocking level of shallow thinking on your part." Roy thinks he is being clever by shielding the personal jab by pretending he is talking about the idea. However, it is pretty clear to the recipient of Roy's remark that it is a personal jab.

Roy needs to understand that how we behave towards one another impacts how well the company functions. One of the elements of structure is that the behaviors serve a purpose in the business to promote the right results. A violation of those behaviors undermines the company's ability to achieve those results. If Roy continually repeats this behavior it indicates that he does not 'stand corrected'. He must be coached by peers to refrain from such behaviors (or go behave elsewhere).

Within the Roy example we may have a bigger problem. We know we can correct his behavior. However, behavior is only half the equation. Behind that behavior we want Roy to be highly motivated. Perhaps he delivers the behaviors, but something about those behaviors goes against his grain. Roy's peer group will be expected to face this concern and resolve it.

In the weekly Rated 10 meeting, when it is Roy's turn to be the subject of the Team Member Focus, as other members of the team report on his motivation, they will question his inclination and ability to find *Identity* and *Meaning* in the work. Roy's behavior will become a concern. When we deal with a concern we lay it all out on the table. Roy will want to take a little time to determine if he can truly be motivated to exhibit the right behaviors since the evidence makes it apparent that this currently may not be the case. If Roy recognizes that he is unable to be self-motivated when exhibiting the desired behaviors and refraining from banned behaviors then the right thing for him, and for the company is for Roy to find work where he can be truly motivated. Roy should leave the company.

Recently I attended the University of Chicago event where two Northwestern University Kellogg graduates spoke. One of them was Robert Pasin, CEO of Radio Flyer, the red wagon we all grew up with. An audience member asked this question, "*So you are growing your company and you make a new hire who doesn't fit into your culture but is very, very good at what he does and makes a lot of money. So who wins the culture or the superstar?"*

Without a moment's hesitation Robert Pasin responded, "The culture. That's very easy. We learned that the hard way, with a superstar that nobody could work with. Whenever that happens we have a program called 'Deselection With Dignity' and we mean it because we want to part ways in such a way that everyone feels good about themselves and Radio Flyer."

If an employee cannot abide the behaviors needed by the business then that employee is not earning his or her pay. Any behavior that is inconsistent with the behavior established by the company is unworthy of pay. If that behavior impacts others in a negative way, as it did in the Radio Flyer example, then it is doubly expensive to the company. Mr Pasin went on to explain that if a sales rainmaker ends up demeaning and aggravating the rest of the team, then that person actually has a net negative impact on the business. Either they correct themselves or they leave.

In most cases we do not make recommendations around specific behaviors. Although when it comes to developing policy to support structure we do make one recommendation. Include in your policy a requirement that all conversations around behavior be conducted on an adult-to-adult basis. Typically these conversations can be emotionally charged. As long as one of you stays on the adult level the other party will eventually come around to that level as well. And, it is as adults that the damage will be repaired.

The policy typically includes the notion that anyone can coach anyone else when it comes to behavior. We set the behavioral standard and it applies to everyone! If a behavior is ok for one person, it is ok for everyone. If a behavior is banned for one person it is banned for everyone. No exceptions. That means the customer service clerk is allowed to point out a banned behavior even to the CEO.

When it comes to policy, less is more. As we have a penchant to make things more complex, we also seem to have a penchant for creating policies.

> *I worked for a large bank that had volumes of policies that were not always consistent. The problem got so big that one day an ad hoc group formed made up of interested volunteers from various business units to try to come up with a way to address the issue. One of the things they did was create a new policy that said no new policies could be created without approval of the Policies Committee. This policy was never approved by the Policies Committee since no such committee existed.*

Structure for Delivery

The discipline of *Peer-to-Peer Accountability* only works when you have two or more people getting together. This is a meeting.

Thus, the structure for delivery under a *Peer-to-Peer Accountability* model consists of a series of very effective and efficient meetings. That is where the discipline of accountability happens.

We use a set of four meeting types to manage the business.
1. The Daily Meetings
2. Weekly Rated 10 Meetings
3. Quarterly Goal Setting Meetings
4. Annual Plan Meetings

The Daily Meetings

I was introduced to the daily meeting back in 1974 working as an American adviser in a Iranian military hangar in Isfahan Iran. First thing every morning the maintenance chief would gather all the guys for a 5 to 10 minute meeting. Forty of us would crowd into the avionics lab, most of us standing or leaning up against a work bench and Larry, our boss, would get our day started. It usually began with something humorous. Sometimes it would be something sad. Then Larry would lay out any key priorities for the day and we'd get to work.

Set a specific time to meet every day. I've always done this first thing in the morning when the work day starts. People may join by phone if they are away on business. There is no excuse for missing a meeting except if you are out sick, on vacation, or dead.

This should be a large group meeting, everyone in the office attending, including the warehouse. The most senior person runs the meeting. There is nothing wrong with using good humor as the tone for these meetings. You want people to look forward to these meetings.

It is a short meeting. We suggest 10 minutes. Vern Harnish suggests that you should not use the short daily meetings for problem solving. We agree except for quick kill problems where someone needs information and doesn't know where to go. Many such problems, can be solved on the spot. Otherwise, if the problem requires work, and is not immediately urgent, it can go up on a team's *CIPIO List* (see below). These meetings are a good place to raise *concerns* but not usually solve them. Often someone else will have had the same concern in the past and can tell you how they solved it.

If you develop a problem with absenteeism or tardiness here is a trick I learned a few years ago. Establish standing teams of 4 employees. These can be cross-departments teams to help people get to know one another. At the beginning of each meeting ask a trivia question. (Before you ask the question you can announce how many points it is worth and you should vary the points values.) The team records its answer on a sheet of paper and turns it in. If they get the question right, they earn the points. However, if a team member is missing (other than an excused absence) then the team cannot earn points for that meeting. Have a periodic prize of nominal value for accumulated points during the period.

The Rated 10 Weekly Meeting
This is a well tested weekly meetings agenda. It is adapted from Verne Harnish and Gino Wickman. Here is the agenda:
> Check-in
> The Numbers
> New Customer and Team *Concerns*
> Team Member Focus
> Concern Resolution
> Rate the Meeting

Verne suggest that you schedule the meeting for the same time slot and same place every week. The meeting should last an hour and a half and as Gino Wickman requires, it should <u>start and end on-time!</u>

We already talked about the Check-in. It is the piece each of personal and business good news that everyone reports at the start of the meeting.

We also talked about the Team Member Focus in the *Peer-to-Peer Accountability* section earlier. This is where you help a single member of the team deliver the right behaviors and find good *Identity* and *Meaning* in their work.

The Numbers

The second part of the weekly meeting we also take from
Verne. In this part of the meeting you are reporting 'the
numbers'. Every team should use a scoreboard[30] to track their
key performance indicators (KPI). These are SMART[31] goals.
For the team as a whole there should be five to fifteen
measurable weekly goals. Every employee should have at least 1
measurable. For each individual, the Scoreboard numbers they
are responsible for are added to the Colleague Letter of
Commitments.

To the extent possible, these numbers should be predictive in
nature. For example, imagine it is the salesperson's goal to close
2 deals per week. That means they must have 4 face to face
meeting, 8 phone calls, and 16 prospects. The predictive
measureable is the number of prospects contacted during the
week.

Scoreboard goals display the state of the business or department
for that team. Each measurable has a weekly target number.
Each number must have a single person who is responsible for it
and accountable to the group for the behaviors that deliver that
goal.

Every KPI on the scoreboard belongs to a specific individual.
No KPI's are shared. Sharing goals translates into no
accountability. The Behavioral Advantage™ model is based on
rigorous accountability. When you establish the KPI you want
to specify the behaviors that drive that KPI. In the Behavioral
Advantage™ model we hold people accountable for their

---

[30] We use "Scoreboard" rather than "Scorecard" because a scoreboard is what
professionals use. It is out there in the open. A scorecard is something you can
keep in your pocket. Accountability requires a more public display of your
professional accomplishments.
[31] SMART is an acronym for Specific, Measurable, Attainable, Relevant and
Timely.

behavior. The performance against the KPI is an indicator of the employee's delivery of the defined behavior.

This is a key distinction. Since behavior is all you get, you want to hold people accountable for the behavior. When a KPI is missed we use the *CIPIO redress* methodology described below to determine if the employee isn't producing the prescribed behavior or the behavior itself needs modification.

In the scoreboard portion of the weekly meeting the responsible person reports the number as "met" or "did not meet". In this part of the meeting it is reporting only. No discussion.

Gino Wickman uses this methodology as well as part of his Entrepreneurial Operating System.[32] Anytime a target is missed, it goes up on a list. We call this the *CIPIO List*.

New Customer and Team *Concerns*

This is also reporting only. Any *concerns, issues, problems, ideas, opportunities* that have arisen during the past week are captured on the *CIPIO List*. In turn, you go around the table and ask participants to list any customer *concerns* or any team *concerns*. You do this quickly, no discussion.

To do's

These are action steps that come out of the *CIPIO redress* process described below. You simply report these as well as "Done", or "Not Done", or "Not Done but On Track". If a To Do is reported as Not Done, it goes up on the *CIPIO List*. No discussion.

---

[32] We recommend every company have installed a disciplined operating methodology. Gino Wickman's EOS is the best one we've come across and we like to install it with clients.

90 Day Goals

These goals come out of the Quarterly Goal Setting Meetings (see below). The reporting here is "On Track", "Off Track" or "Done!" If a goal is Off Track it goes up on the *CIPIO List*.

Team Member Focus

We described this process in the *Peer-to-Peer Accountability* chapter earlier. If there are *concerns* that arise through the discussion, they go up on the *CIPIO List*. After you've spent a few minutes focusing on this week's team member and evaluating their behavior and motivation, you move into resolving *concerns*.

CIPIO redress

You begin by prioritizing the top three items on the *CIPIO List*. You need only prioritize the top three items because you may not get through the whole list and you are better off using the meeting time to redress concerns. Moreover, some of the items on the list may not represent a level of concern to warrant redress yet. For example take the scoreboard goal for your salesperson to contact 16 prospects per week. Suppose that team member reports, "Did not meet," and the actual number is 15 on the report. As an isolated incident, missing the goal by one may not warrant any action by the peer group. However, if the target had been missed three weeks in a row, the priority would likely be higher.

The top priority *concern* is taken down from the list and put on the table for redress. Your objective is to redress the *concern* and permanently remove it from the Weekly *CIPIO List* (which carries over week to week).

When solving a *concern* you want to first follow the causal chain to find the root cause. The root cause is the real source of *concern.* Often an item on the list will be described as a symptom rather than the real nature of the *concern.* You can utilize the 5 why's technique here as well. Keep in mind that the root cause will link back to behavior most of the time. This is a time for open, honest dialogue with everyone around the table getting an opportunity to contribute to the discussion. It is not about blame.

Once the team agrees that you've identified the real nature of the *concern* you should know what caused it. It could be an unanticipated external factor got in the way of the person doing the right behaviors for this deliverable. It also could be bad luck. It could be that the person responsible did not perform the desired behaviors for this KPI. If the person did exhibit the right behaviors and the results were not as expected, then perhaps the definition of the behavior needs to be re-evaluated. Whatever the cause, you go around the table with each person contributing to the discussion on how to redress the *concern.*. Usually, the resolution of a *concern* results in additional to-dos. All to-dos are SMART goals assigned to specific individuals.

Once the first *concern* is resolved you move on to the next one until the scheduled amount time for the meeting is almost up. Any item left on the *CIPIO List* is carried over to the next meeting. You may remove an item from the list either by resolving it or by agreeing that it is no longer a *concern*.

Rate the Meeting
Verne Harnish suggest you end the meeting by going around the table asking each team member to sum up the meeting in a word or phrase. We prefer Gino Wickman's method. You rate how the team did in the meeting on a scale of 1(waste of time)-10(great meeting).

We use this with clients as well. Before you schedule your first Rated 10 meeting, you ask team members to rate the effectiveness of their current staff meetings on a scale of 1 to 10. Typically, honest answers will rate the old meetings somewhere between 3 and 6. The goal is to achieve ratings that approach 10s, hence the meetings are called Rated 10 meetings.

One team I know of, in honor of the movie Spinal Tap, changed the scale used from 1-10 to 1-11. They said they we going to have even better meetings than mere '10s'. We encourage you to have some fun in these meetings. Most of our clients look forward to these meetings each week; they get stuff done, and it is an hour and a half of good camaraderie. Make them enjoyable!

End the meeting on time.

Quarterly Goal Setting Meetings

We use a quarterly meeting at the leadership level to review the prior 90 Day goals, and to set the new 90 Day Mission. The goals set by the leadership team for the next 90 days will cascade down through the organization to form the basis for how each person establishes their individual 90 Day goals. Each peer group also has a quarterly meeting to review prior performance and set new goals.

Annual Plan Meetings

These are leadership team meeting in which the prior year accomplishments are reviewed, the direction for the coming year is set, and the next 90 Day Mission is established. When you implement something like EOS, you will discover there is much more to the Annual Plan Meeting.

The One Page Strategic Plan

Verne Harnish and Gino Wickman both recommend a one page strategic plan. This is a necessity. When it comes to behavior and motivation it is very important that people can keep your strategic plan in mind. It must be easy to grasp and easy to remember. For humans it is always a challenge to keep things succinct when we are close to a topic. We tend to over-communicate the details because we think they matter. While the details are important to those who must think it through thoroughly, everyone else only needs the high points. Be brief. To make the strategic plan accessible it is wise to break the information down into groups of threes. It is easier to remember things when they are grouped in threes (and sometimes, fours).

The goal is to have your employees to keep in mind: What you do; Why you're doing it; and How you do it.

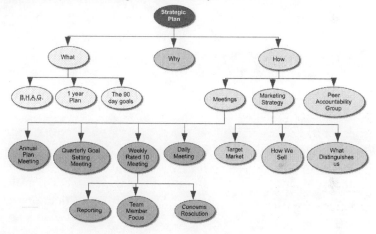

What We Do.

This is a simple short statement about what you do. For example: *"We're here to make plumbing products that work."* The What We Do portion of the strategic plan includes the Big Hairy Audacious Goal (B.H.A.G.) that Jim Collins and Jerry Porras introduced in *Built to Last*. This is the far distant lighthouse you're sailing toward. It's a statement of where you want the company to be in ten or fifteen years. When you do this, it is simply a picture of where you are located, how many people work there, how many customers do you have, what is your geographic reach, what is your revenue, what is your profit, and what is the B.H.A.G. achievement date.

The One Year Plan is what you are going to do in the next four quarters to move toward that B.H.A.G. You do this once per year. You can adjust it only once, and it is during your next Quarterly Goal Setting Meeting. The One Year Plan should contain a revenue, and profit component as well as any new market directions. It should also include 3 to 7 key goals for the year that will put you on track to make the B.H.A.G.

The last component of 'What We Do' is the list of 90 day goals for this quarter. For the business, you will typically establish 3 to 7 goals that move the business forward in the direction of the One Year Goal. Each of these goals is assigned to an individual; typically someone on the leadership team. These goals cascade down through the business and form the basis for Division, Department, and team goals.

In addition to the business goals, there may be a set of one to three individual goals for each person on any team at every level of the company. These are also 90 day (13 weeks) goals. Progress against them is part of the reporting section of the weekly Rated 10 Meeting.

Why We're Doing It
'Why We're Doing It' is our reason for being. It is our Core Ideology which we will talk about earlier. We will defined both elements of the Core Ideology, the purpose and the values of the company. They provide handholds for employees to find their own purpose and motivation that helps them to articulate what *Identity* and *Meaning* they will derive from the work.

How We Do It

We have already discussed the meetings structure briefly: The Annual Planning Meeting, The Quarterly Goal Setting Meeting, the Weekly Rated 10 Meeting, and the Daily Meeting. These form the backbone of the 'How We Do It' part of the strategic plan. We have also talked about the *Peer-to-Peer Accountability* group and how it plays a central role in leading behavior and sustaining motivation. That leaves the last element of the one page Strategic Plan – The Marketing Strategy.

The Marketing Strategy is made up of three sections. The first section is where you define your target market. Like the rest of the Strategic Plan, the target market gets reviewed and restated during every Annual Planning Meeting and it may be updated during the Quarterly Goal Setting Meeting. Young companies often accept any customer who comes across the transom. Sometimes these turn out to be the wrong customers and need to go. Defining the Target Market is about going after the right customers.

How you define the Target Market depends upon the nature of your business. For some companies the target will consist of specific demographics and psychographics. When considering demographics you will look at: age; gender; ethnic background; marital status; family status; income level; education level; occupation; and location. For psychographic considerations you will look at: behavior; lifestyles; values; attitudes; personality; interests and hobbies; appetites; and relationships.

For other companies it is more useful to specify exact targets. These are specific customers you want to acquire. As consultants, we often define a list of specific companies where we think we can add significant value based on where they are and what we do.

The second section of the marketing strategy is to define how you sell. This consists of your process for marketing and selling to your target market. Gino Wickman talks about his father's proven process. He recommends a single sheet of paper that shows the steps you take with a prospect from the first meeting through the life of the relationship. We use a similar tool; a two sided sheet of heavy card stock. On one side is the Behavioral Advantage™ six slice pie graphic. It provides the basis for us to talk about what we do and why it matters to our customer. The other side displays the steps we go through to deliver the product. This is also where you would mention your guarantee and how it is meaningful to the customer. Not every business needs a guarantee to enhance their ability to sell, where it gives you an edge, you should have one.

Finally, the third element of the Marketing Strategy is what distinguish you from your competition in the eyes of your customers. It is a list of the three or four things that make you unique. Here, what you think doesn't matter; it is all about your customer. It is helpful to talk to some of your best customers and ask them why they choose you over your competition. This is a precious list and one that provides guidance on how you want your people to behave. Employee behavior should support and enhance these distinguishers.

The Strategic Plan document
Every employee has their own copy of the Strategic Plan. It will include their personal goals for the next 90 day period. It is updated every quarter in the Quarterly Goal Setting Meeting.

XYZ COMPANY
STRATEGIC PLAN

NAME _____   DATE: _____

XYZ CORE IDEOLOGY

OUR PURPOSE

OUR VALUES

XYZ MARKETING STRATEGY

TARGET

SALES PROCESS

WHAT DISTINGUISHES XYZ

GOALS

B.H.A.G.
REVENUE

PROFIT

DUE DATE _____

ONE YEAR PLAN
REVENUE

PROFIT

DUE DATE _____

NEXT 13 WEEKS
REVENUE

PROFIT

DUE DATE _____

PERSONAL 90 DAY GOALS   DUE DATE _____

Empowerment

The last core element of Structure is the final piece we implement with companies. It is the structure around empowerment.

To continue to get employees to give you their discretionary thinking and deliver ideas that boost margin, you must empower them to implement their ideas. Empowerment is about giving employees the 'power' to deliver changes. Empowered employees are authorized and enabled to do what they determine is needed to achieve company goals.

For a CEO this can be scary stuff. What happens if an employee gets an idea to build a perpetual motion machine, which violates the laws of physics! Do you let that employee pursue an obviously flawed idea? The answer to that question is the marketing answer: "It depends!" Sometimes the by-product of a crazy idea is a great idea. As you'll see in a moment, we do put a governor on ideas, which makes it less likely that truly stupid ideas will be pursued.

Explicit empowerment is key. At Gore "teams organize around opportunities and leaders emerge." We've seen that 3M pioneered the idea of giving employees the ability to set aside time to work on special projects. Google gives its engineers *20 percent time*, so that they're free to work on what they're really passionate about. Google's belief in empowerment can be summed up as, "give the proper tools to a group of people who like to make a difference, and they will."[33] Likewise, Toyota did this with the employees in the famous NUMMI assembly plant. And today, Morning Star employees clearly enjoy this level of empowerment.

---

[33] Google corporate site, "Our Philosophy", Accessed 11/14/2009 http://www.google. com/corporate/tenthings.html

Unfortunately, lots of large companies use stage-gate processes to control ideas. Stage-gate processes are about reducing risk, but they can kill innovation. Until recently, there was a large mobile phone manufacturer in the town where I live. It employed a rigid stage-gate process. In a conversation with one of its engineers, he told me about an idea a colleague of his came up with. The trouble was the idea was far enough removed from the mobile phone model that the stage-gate process did not fit. The process killed the idea in the early stage. The stage-gate methodology is all about setting-up roadblocks. You do want to control risk, but you also want to remove roadblocks.

One blanket way to minimize early stage risk is the *20 percent time* solution. The 20 percent time is a way to allow early stage risks to be contained to this small package of an individual's time. It works well at Google because development work often can be pursued by an individual or a small cooperating team.

W.L. Gore & Associates uses an approach which allows ideas to bubble up until a team is needed to take it to the next level. As the need for additional resources increases, the team grows.

At 3M, the CEO who nearly killed the idea for masking tape recognized the limitations in his own ability to recognize a good idea and that an employee with a passion should be allowed to pursue an idea. This approach paid off in 1968, when Spencer Silver discovered his unique adhesive that Art Fry, later turned into Post-it® Notes. It took eight years for the Post-it® Notes to reach the market. This story illustrates how much time may pass, from having an idea to bringing it to market.

If Art Fry had to go through a stage-gate process for his 'hymnal bookmark', (the inspiration for Post-it® Notes) the process would have required a business plan with business goals, a market analysis, financial analysis, technical evaluation, and competitive research. (These requirements are taken from the "front end" of an actual stage gate process.) You can almost hear someone kill the idea with, "Look, if there were any kind of market for hymnal bookmarks, someone would already be in that space. It's a nonstarter."

A key to allowing people to pursue ideas is to establish a flexible Risk-gate™ process. This process facilitates the least expensive, but best use of resources to pass an idea through primary risks. The basic purpose of the flexible Risk-gate™ process is to vet the idea in terms of what knowledge is missing. Select the next easiest, cheapest, but meaningful risk to resolve and come up with a strategy to remove that risk. Such risks could be about what form factor a product should have, or will customers accept the product,—or perhaps a prototype is needed; or perhaps a manufacturing step is needed that's never been done before—find a way to test the step or develop alternatives; or perhaps you don't know if the technology will work when it's put together with other parts—test building a working model.

This leaves the issue of deciding which ideas to pursue. The best way to do this is to implement a method that removes management from the decision altogether. Asking management for permission is equivalent to asking for a 'no'. Managers often have no motivation for taking on the risk and employees often will get an answer like "We already tried that and it didn't work." Take this true story:

Two scientists set out to look into the biological processes for making proteins. Ribosomes have the job of linking amino acids together as instructed by messenger RNA for a particular protien. The scientists suggested that ribosomes would respond to whatever RNA was provided. They designed an experiment to take ribosomes from bacteria and insert into them the messenger RNA from peas. Would they would grow pea proteins or bacteria proteins? Had the experiment worked, they would have been the first to demonstrate the uniformity of life. But the experiment simply didn't work at all.

You can easily imagine someone coming along later to attempt to do the same thing getting the response "We already tried that and it didn't work!" Chris Galvin, the former CEO of Motorola, described how he and his father would deal with this kind of question. If someone came to him with an idea that had already been tried, the Motorola CEO wouldn't say, "We already tried that." Instead, he would encourage the innovator to pursue the idea and give some guidance where to look first. If the reason the idea didn't work the first time was valid, the innovator would see the problem fairly soon, report the issue back to Galvin, and then go off to pursue some other idea.

If you just shoot an idea down with "we already tried that," then you make it very difficult for that person to move off that idea and onto a new one. They will keep thinking about it, believing the people that went before them just didn't see the problem right, or perhaps made some error. They will waste a lot more time thinking about this problem than they would have if they'd been allowed to work on it. A side problem is that you also diminish their level of engagement.

In the case of the ribosomes RNA experiment, eventually someone did come along and show the uniformity of life. The reason the original experiment failed was due to the amateurish contribution of the lab assistant. The bacteria ribosomes he brought to the experiment, were some he'd developed in a previous experiment and had stored for some time in a lab refrigerator. While there, they'd become contaminated and unusable which caused the experiment to fail. Who was this lab assistant? It was Richard Feynman, the renown physicist and Nobel Laureate. Just because something has been tried before, doesn't mean there's no value in trying again. And just because it was tried by someone who's incredibly smart, doesn't mean an error didn't occur.

You can take out the need for management decisions by establishing a flexible Risk-gate™ funding pool.

The governor here is that no-one can get funding without getting at least one other employee to sign onto the idea. You limit the number of ideas any individual can sign onto in a six month period. Employees will only sign onto projects which they deem worthy, thus you build in a certain level of control. Will you have ideas that fail? Of course you will. But just letting the employee pursue the idea is a far better factor of engagement than paying an annual bonus, and far cheaper.

The amount of funding available depends on the nature of the business. For some businesses it might be $5,000 for others $500. If more money is needed as risks are eliminated, then more people must join the project. If you got $500 when two people joined perhaps you fund an additional $500 when a third signs on and an additional 1,000 when a fourth joins, and so on.

A flexible risk gate process enables you to establish project-specific milestones while remaining flexible about what those milestones are and who needs to be involved. The employees involved identify what the next critical risk factor is, and determine what they must overcome and which approach has the smallest possible investment. Some ideas need a couple of hundred dollars to move to the next stage, but others may need thousands. The mantra for all employees is to preserve cash and look for creative ways to move an idea along without creating an unnecessary financial risk.

Along the same lines is something we call the CEO Passion Pool™. This is an alternate funding source controlled solely by the CEO. This provides a pathway to employees when they are unsuccessful in getting anyone else interested in their idea. Plus, sometimes an employee will have such a good idea that it should be held close to the vest for a while. Employees can approach the CEO for funding for their idea, and at her sole discretion, the CEO may provide the requested funds.

Each CEO will naturally create his or her own criteria for funding an idea from the CEO Passion Pool™. The CEO must keep in mind that his or her own mindset could filter out the best ideas. History has repeatedly shown that senior management does a poor job of judging ideas.

Since it is called the Passion Pool™ perhaps the best criterion is the level of passion the creator has for the idea. Normally it takes a good deal of personal commitment for anyone to approach the CEO. If the creator can articulate the problem and the solution then you at least have some notion of the potential for the idea. Perhaps a good reminder is that ideas like a hymnal bookmark hardly seem powerful or even worthwhile.

Robert Galvin, the CEO of Motorola, back when the company was an innovation powerhouse, suggested that trusting a person's passions is an act of faith that "things are doable that are not necessarily provable." Galvin was a strong advocate of trust, engagement, and empowerment. Because the CEO can pull in needed resources, the idea can be vetted, not for its inherent value, but to determine the next, least-expensive, reasonable step. This keeps the idea alive but limits the investment risk to the minimal next step.

Empowerment is the last of the core elements of Behavioral Advantage™ we implement with companies. First they must get the right behaviors, the right motivators, implement *Peer-to-Peer Accountability*, and get good at delivery and resolving concerns. Where the company is large enough, we provide a software tool that enables the business to run and control the Risk-gate™ and Passion Pool™

Part 2

Part 2 is designed specifically for the Human Relations manager.

HR Advantage

The objective of this chapter is to give the HR (Human Relations) department the tools to take more ownership of hiring. If you are outsourcing your HR functions, make sure you outsource to a company that can fulfill this role. Give them this part of the book and ask them if they can do what it asks in this chapter. If not, find another firm.

One time I was presenting *The Peak Interview* to a group of 'in transition' senior corporate executives. In the discussion session following the talk, one of the executives mentioned that he was always mystified why the hiring manager played the decision-maker role in the hiring process. The hiring manager may interact with the 'new hire' for a relatively short time as compared to their total time with the company. In most cases, leaders don't get to hire their team members. More commonly, they inherit their people from their predecessor. Great leaders take the people they get and turn them into a great team.

The better model for the company is to leave the talent acquisition to the experts in HR.

'The sign reminded me of our interview with Walter Bruckart, vice president during the good-to-great years. When asked to name the top five factors that led to the transition from mediocrity to excellence, Bruckart said, 'One would be people. Two would be people. Three would be people. Four would be people. And five would be people. A huge part of our transition can be attributed to our discipline in picking the right people.' (J. Collins, Good to Great 2001)

Fire the hiring manager?

Every aspect of your competitive advantage comes from your people and their behavior. The leadership team is going to focus on behaviors and motivators; that's probably 80% of the battle.

The other 20% is the lift you get by employing the right talent. Companies that employ people who can work together while thinking differently tend to be better at defining problems. The better they are at accurately defining problems, the better they'll be at creating new opportunities for growth. Implementing great new solutions that create competitive advantage with customers is called 'innovation'. Diversity of mind and the behaviors that leverage it are the keystones of an innovative human capital structure. This is the foundation of a sustainable competitive advantage.

Why is it that when companies reach out to hire the best candidates, they do such a mediocre job of hiring for diversity of mind?

The research here is definitive, "Hiring managers hire the people they like the most."

Why do hiring managers hire the people they like the most? It's because hiring managers have a tendency to see themselves as very capable to master the tasks associated with the open position. After all, it is a subordinate role to the role they play. In many cases it is a job they once held. Candidates who remind hiring managers of themselves are people whom the hiring manager will see as being capable of doing the job. It turns out that we like people who are similar to us. Unfortunately, this practice does not deliver diversity of mind.

By the time a person has made it to the interview with the hiring manager, the company has thoroughly screened the candidates for the required skills, knowledge, abilities, competencies, education and experience. Thus, when the hiring manager chooses the person he or she likes the most, the person will likely be a competent employee. In other words, almost any of these people could step into the job. Even though the person the hiring manager likes best is usually a good fit for the hiring manager, it is often not the best choice for the company overall. The company does not need people who all think alike.

What's the Value of an Interview?

It turns out that even if hiring managers had ample job interview training, they would still be ineffective. Research abounds to show job interviews, even ones conducted by professionals (psychologists, professional recruiters, HR managers) do not achieve the results we like to believe they do. As we will see shortly, a Texas University incident accidentally, and dramatically, proved the worthlessness of even a highly structured and discipline professional interviewing process. Before we go to Texas, lets look as some other research.

In 1998, Frank Schmidt and John Hunter published a study of the validity of employment selection methods. In this often quoted study, Schmidt and Hunter examined the validity of 19 selection methods for predicting how well the candidate would perform in the job. Not only did they examine the validity of these methods used in isolation, but also the validity of paired combinations of General Mental Ability (GMA) with the other 18 methods. The selection methods they looked at included formal and informal assessment methods such as:

1. GMA tests
2. Work sample tests
3. Integrity tests
4. Conscientiousness tests
5. Employment interviews (structured)
6. Employment interviews (unstructured)
7. Job knowledge tests
8. Job tryout procedure
9. Peer ratings
10. Training & Experience behavioral consistency method
11. Reference checks
12. Job experience (years)
13. Biographical data measures

14. Assessment centers
15. Training & Experience point method
16. Years of education
17. Interests
18. Graphology
19. Age

In isolation, none of these did a good job. The top three stand-alone methods were 1) work sample tests, 2) employment interviews (structured) and 3) General Mental Ability (GMA) test. The three worst individual predictors of success had no relevance. They were 1) years of education, 2) graphology (handwriting analysis) and 3) age. The results did show that a structured interview was slightly more valid than an unstructured interview. However, while the structured interview was better than the unstructured interview the study found the structured interview was no more valid than a flip of the coin. It turns out that what makes the job interview ineffective is the role our hidden biases play in evaluating people. We will come to biases in a moment.

The Schmidt and Hunter study also examined the combination of the GMA test with other methods. They found that when you combine the General Mental Ability test with the other top methods (work sample tests, and the structured interview) you see an improvement in the predictive value of the methods lifting validity about 25% above the GMA test alone. However, the combination producing the best predictor reported in the Schmidt, Hunter study was the GMA combined with an integrity test. According to the study, you're better off skipping the interview completely and focus instead on hiring the smartest, most honest person in the qualified candidate pool.

You might wonder how someone evaluates the validity of the interview. After all, only one candidate is hired. How would you know if the candidates whom you didn't hire might have performed equally well?

Perhaps the best case which clearly answers that question was the result of a happy accident in Texas. The 'happy' part is that it resulted in 50 candidates being accepted into medical school who otherwise might not have become doctors.

Like most universities, The University of Texas used an interview process to screen applicants for its medical school. It had selected 800 candidates from a pool of 2,200 and brought those 800 applicants onto the Houston campus for interviews. Each candidate was interviewed by a member of the admissions committee as well as a faculty member.

The interviewers then wrote an assessment for each candidate and submitted that to a central committee. Each member of the central committee reviewed each assessment and scored candidates on a scale of 0-7. These scores were averaged and were used to rank all 800 candidates from 1 (best candidate) to 800 (worst candidate). Offers were sent out to the top ranking candidates to fill the 150 vacancies. Many of these top candidates elected to go to other schools. The University of Texas was able to fill the 150 vacancies from the pool of applicants going only as far as the 350th ranked candidate.

Several months later, the Texas state legislature required the University to boost its enrollment from 150 to 200 new medical students. The university medical school now needed an additional 50 students. They sent offers out to the rest of the 800 to fill the 50 spots. However, by this point, most students had already committed to other schools. In the end, they admitted 50 new students who had been ranked in the lowest in the interview scoring scale (700-800).

The school wisely made no distinction once a student was admitted to the program and no-one on the teaching staff knew who were the original 150 and who were the additional 50 students. Did the interview predict better performance successfully? No. There was no difference in performance between the 150 and the 50. By the end of the second year there was no difference in performance in the classroom; by the end of their clinical training, no difference; after their first year of residency; no difference. In the end, 82% of both groups received their MD. Once they had pre-qualified the 800 applicants, the interviews added no value to the selection process. It turns out that some very capable people don't interview well.

Bias

Why do we keep doing something even after we are exposed to evidence that it is not as effective as we thought? We talked about this earlier in the chapter on leadership. Many studies have shown that repetition of any behavior impacts the brain. The psychologist Edward Tolman showed, this happens irrespective of the longevity of the success of the behavior. Repetition reinforces behavior.

The way our brains work limits our ability to see an opportunity for change. For example, study after study has shown that the management of people based on displays of power are the least effective way to gain employee productivity. Yet companies continue to permit such behavior throughout management ranks.

Sometimes when research points in one direction we reject the general conclusion as it applies specifically to us. The truth is, we continue to use the job interview because we continue to believe that we are the exception; we are the rare people who are good at it.

The reason the job interview is not effective is due to bias. Psychologists have shown two things about bias: First, we cannot keep our own biases in check. Second, we are unaware of what goes into our personal biases. You may think you are a great interviewer, unfortunately, you cannot detect or eliminate your own bias. This is as true for the poorly trained hiring manager as it is for the musician with a great ear for music, or as it is for the clinical psychologist (although the latter hates to admit it and takes pains to try to overcome it).

"It took me very little time (less than 5 minutes) to determine whether or not a particular candidate would be suitable for the job. It wasn't just his/her physical appearance or actions but also the first verbal interactions we had."

This was a statement made by an HR manager in a comment responding to a blog of a Stanford professor. We all believe we are good at sizing-up someone within the first few moments of meeting them and our subsequent interaction with the person almost always proves us right. The human brain plays lots of tricks on us, and this sizing-up and subsequent confirmation of that sizing-up are two of them.

The rapid sizing-up of a person is called 'thin-slicing'. The biases at work in our brains when we thin-slice someone usually include a bias called "Anchoring". This bias causes us to weigh one or two quick observations about the person too heavily in our sizing-up process. Subsequently, we cement that evaluation through another bias called "confirmation bias". Confirmation bias causes us to ignore evidence that's inconsistent with how we initially judged the person and over-value consistent evidence. As a result we continue to think we're right about the person.

Thin-slicing is part of face-to-face human interaction. Most of us have experienced someone misjudging us in this manner. Once done, it is very powerful. It is very difficult to get them to see you as you actually are. The more you try, the more you're helping them confirm they were right in the first place.

Allowing anchoring and confirmation bias to foul the hiring process is hardly an effective or professional way to operate a business. Your hiring managers are very confident in their ability to pick the best candidate using the interview process. You would have a tough time convincing them that their confidence is a cognitive illusion, however, that is exactly what it is. There is a better way, a more professional way.

Remember earlier we talked about Kahneman's experience with evaluating cadets for officer training. Each time, the feedback of actual performance should have convinced them that their confidence in their predictions was misplaced; yet it did not. This is useful to keep in mind. When your hiring managers express their confidence in making the hiring decision it is that same cognitive illusion as it was for the Nobel Prize Laureate Dr. Kahneman and for the many admissions experts in the Texas medical school process.

Bias exposed
When a symphony orchestra has a vacancy for a musician it will call for auditions to fill that vacancy. Their selection criterion is very simple: hire the musician who plays the instrument the best. Typically a panel is formed consisting of the conductor, the concertmaster, a number of principal players from the orchestra, as well as a representative of the musicians' union. The panel has a simple mission: listen, then hire the musician who performs the music the best.

Historically, especially in Europe, when the first round of auditions were held, the musician would walk out onto the stage and be required to play a set of defined compositions. Invariably, after the first round of auditions very few people on the call-back sheet were women.

This looked like gender bias. However, if you pointed this out to a member of the panel, you would get an answer like, "I agree, it looks like gender bias, but it is not. We listen very careful to the music. In the end, it is true, it is usually men who produce better musical quality. However, it is the music that decides the matter, not bias."

The reasons given for the male superiority varied from being due to the male's general larger body and greater strength; to an assertion that men have a deeper primal connection to the music; to a belief that men play the music strictly for fun, while women focus on art, and thus their music lacks life. Of course, it's all nonsense.

As a result of discrimination lawsuits, orchestras implemented the blind audition. This method eliminated all signals to the panel as to the gender of the musician. Oddly, it greatly improved women's musical ability! When 50% of the musicians in the first round were women, then the callback sheet would include 50% women.

It is the nature of bias that we cannot detect our own biases. Any effort to overcome bias in ourselves will be fruitless. The only way to avoid a biased decision in the hiring process is to change the way decisions are made. That is what is proposed here. In the end, you will have a much more diverse workforce.

The value of diversity of mind is played out in how problems are defined and solved. When people bring different perspectives to the table and put mental links together differently, you have a better chance to improve synthesis, discovery, and decision-making. The benefits that diversity of thought can bring to business are substantial. Diversity of thought can produce new opportunities to satisfy customers and that increases competitive advantage.

The role of a leader/manager is to get the best possible performance from employees. When a leader steps into a new role, he or she inherits the existing staff. Great leaders rarely make substantial changes to the teams they inherit. Their job is to get the best out of the people they are asked to lead. Compared to HR professionals, leaders have no particular training in choosing the best candidate.

Imagine someone in your company needs a computer. Chances are you don't say to that employee, "Go out on the Internet and do some research; get four or five of your colleagues to look at the choices; and buy the one you like the best." That's probably not what you do. Rather, it is likely you tell your employee to define what functionality she needs and then give that to the IT group and let the experts find the right solution. The computer has to fit into the existing software and hardware environment. So, why do you let this same employee make an amateur decision around acquiring your most important asset, your people? This decision too, should be left to the experts. And that expertise resides with the Human Relations group. HR should be the company experts in hiring and managing the staffing process. This will increase the level of professionalism in a discipline that is very important to the future of the company.

The New Model

In the new model you will no longer use a traditional job interview. Instead you will utilize a disciplined process to ensure you hire the best person for the job <u>and</u> for the company. Whenever a new employee is brought into the organization six criteria/questions must be answered with a "Yes". These questions make sure the candidate: grasps the situation; desires the job; has the ability to master the responsibilities; can produce the required behaviors; feels passion for the role; and has the right character for the company.

(In the diagram above, everything above the middle line has to do with the specified immediate position - the job opening. Everything below the horizontal middle is about fitting into the company.)

ITEM	Description
GRASPS IT	UNDERSTANDS WHAT A WORK DAY WILL BE LIKE: WHO; WHAT; WHERE.
DESIRES IT	PASSION TO CONTRIBUTE, MUCH MORE THAN JUST A PAY-CHECK
MASTERS IT	HAS SKILL, KNOWLEDGE, COMPETENCIES, EXPERIENCE, EDUCATION, ETC.
BEHAVIORS FIT	PERSONAL AND LEADERSHIP BEHAVIORAL TENDENCIES FIT COMPANY CULTURE
PASSION FIT	SHARES THE PASSION FOR THE VISION; SHARES 'WHY' & "HOW"
CHARACTER FIT	HAS THE CHARACTER TRAITS DEEMED ESSENTIAL TO THE COMPANY

Grasps It

Does the candidate get it? Does the candidate understand the environment he or she is about to step into? Does the candidate have a 'feel' for the position? This is a step that is very often skipped in the selection process. If it is handled at all, it will be after an offer has been made and the candidate wants to find out more about the specific job. The purpose of the *Grasps It* step is to ensure that the candidate has an accurate picture of what it will be like to work in the company in the specific position for which they will be hired. The reason this matters is that the next question, *Desires It* cannot be answered unless you are sure the candidate *Grasps It*. How can a candidate know they want something, if they don't understand what that something is?

A focus of Behavioral Advantage™ is behavior. Thus, an important component of the *Grasps It* step is to verify that the candidate understands what behaviors are needed for the specific job.

The HR representative should meet with members of the functional team to create a list of what the team considers to be the critical behaviors, interactions, activities and functions for the position. The HR representative will create a Behavioral Grid tailored for the specific position (see the chapters on Behavior and Motivation). This grid will prioritize the key behaviors. HR will also make a list of the key day-to-day interactions, and a qualitative understanding of how they occur, what transpires, and their purposes. The HR representative needs to know how long and steep the learning curve will be. The HR representative should have an understanding of the tone of the environment; is it intense, relaxed, fun, stressful, etc.?

To properly execute this step the candidate should either shadow someone in the department, or meet with the HR representative who will brief the candidate on the day-to-day interactions. This should be followed by the candidate summarizing his or her understanding of the required behaviors and the environment, either to the HR person or some other relevant personnel. This is an education exercise, not an evaluative exercise. The HR representative needs to feel that the candidate has a good understanding of what the work environment will be like in order to proceed to the *Desires It* step. Your goal is to make sure the candidate understands the situation.

Desires It

In the *Desires It* step you will make sure the candidate is applying for the job for a good reason...not out of desperation.

Does the candidate actually want the job? Studies, even conservative studies, have found that engaged employees cause: high retention rates, better financial performance, and higher customer loyalty.

A candidate whose only interest in the job is the paycheck will be a hard-to-engage employee. To truly engage an employee, the individual needs to be someone who can create *Identity* and

Meaning from the work and the environment. It must be someone who truly wants the job.

The single most important element here is the behavior element. Does the candidate actually want to perform the key behaviors for the role. For example, imagine that you are hiring for a sales position. You've identified two high priority behaviors for the job; one for closing a sale and one for prospecting a sale. In the course of the conversation you find out that the candidate loves closing and hates prospecting. Since you've identified both as key behaviors; you must fill the role with someone who wants to do both.

Ask the candidate why he or she wants the job. The candidate may struggle a bit to answer this question. He or she may talk about the great reputation of the company, or that its is a great a place to build a career, or even about how it's the right job. Let the candidate talk, don't be afraid of silence.

You can ask follow-up questions like, "In thinking about this job, what about it excites you?" If the candidate cannot present a convincing description of why the job is interesting and desirable, then the candidate may not be the right person for the job.

What you want to hear in the candidate's voice is genuine desire and energy. The more evident these are, the more likely the person will be engaged in the work.

Masters It

The candidate must have the basic qualifications to perform the job function. These qualifications represent the capacity to do the job and include: skills, knowledge, abilities, competencies, experience and education required for the job for which the candidate is being considered.

In today's hiring process, with hundreds of resumes coming in for an open position, a good filtering process ensures that anyone who makes it as far as the job interview has the qualifications for the job. The filtering process does a reasonably good job of selecting such candidates.

If we remove the hiring manager's interviewing role, what is left is greater emphasis on the method that defines the requirements for this job. One of the most frequent complaints we hear from executives in transition is how poorly companies construct job descriptions. If defining the job requirements is done poorly, it will be difficult to do a good job of evaluating candidates in terms of the capabilities needed for the job.

This calls for a rigorous process of discovering, rationalizing and articulating the requirements. The hiring manager plays a big role here, and other employees may also be needed to discover all the job requirements. HR should also ask the functional manager what would make for outstanding performance in the job.

The role of HR is to make sure the business unit does not set the bar higher than necessary and that the job is doable. For example, don't require ten years of experience when 98% of the necessary knowledge is found in someone with one year of experience.

Once the requirements and qualifications are well defined, the process for determining if a candidate possesses the necessary qualifications usually does not require the hiring manager. HR may be able to do this independently. If the qualifications require a level of technical expertise, then an employee who has that expertise can help determine whether or not a candidate has the level of technical ability needed. In a case like this, the interviewing employee is only evaluating the candidate's technical expertise. The process should be rigorous. The evaluation should be scripted to ensure that personality and other sources of bias can have little or no impact. The process should also be consistent; every candidate should be evaluated in the same way.

Usually the resume does a poor job of revealing a candidate's true competencies. Make a list of competencies needed for the job; and then create some behavioral event interview questions that would allow a candidate to reveal those competencies. The key here is to avoid giving away what competencies you're looking for. Avoid asking questions like, "*Tell me about your leadership ability,*" or "*Give me an example of a time when you played a leadership role.*" Instead, ask a question like "*I'm sure you've played significant roles on teams before. Tell me about such a time, what were you trying to accomplish as a team, what happened, and what was your contribution?*" If leadership is what you're looking for and it isn't the contribution the candidate describes, then ask a follow-up, "*Tell me about a time where you played a different role.*" If leadership doesn't emerge here either, most likely it is not a core competency of the individual.

Grasps It, Desires It and *Masters It*, all relate to the specific job at hand. Keep in mind, you are not only hiring for a specific position, you are staffing the company. To do a good job staffing the company you will need additional criteria. This brings us to Company Criteria.

Company Criteria

Beyond being a fit for the job, the candidate must also be a fit for the company. An employee's alignment with the company's purpose and values can impact the motivation of that employee. Likewise, it is important to hire people who share the personal character of the ideal employee.

The most important goal is to hire people who will behave in the manner needed to operate successfully in the company. While it is the most important, fortunately it is not the most difficult criterion to meet. That's because most people behave according to the environment they find themselves in. In Behavioral Advantage™ we deliberately manage this environment.

We started this chapter by saying, "Diversity of mind and the behaviors that leverage it are the keystones of an innovative human capital structure." Diversity of mind is a characteristic that describes the broad portfolio of people in the organization. However, it is at the individual level where the organization derives its power. The company's competitive advantage is determined by how well it solves customer and operating problems as compared to the competition. These problems are found in every nook and cranny of the business from marketing and sales, through operations, customer service, finance, IT, and HR.

Humans have an enormous capacity to solve complex problems. What determines the depth and quality of problem solving is persistence. Persistence is determined by the individual's self-motivation to stick with the problem. Persistence will take place only when the employee is fully engaged in the work. Engagement is often discussed in terms of discretionary effort. However, "effort" is the wrong word in this case because it implies an earnestness in the amount of exertion expended for a specified purpose. In fact, the power is found in discretionary **thinking**, For the highly engaged person, this discretionary thinking is **effortless**. The employee engages in this thinking because solving the problem provides *Identity* and *Meaning* for the employee. It is a work of love.

HR plays a pivotal role in ensuring there is a company fit. Everyone knows that the 'right' answer to any interview question is the one the company wants to hear. We want to dig deep to get to the real answers.

Passion Fit

In part one of this book we talked about Core Ideology. It consists of the core purpose and the core values. The Core Ideology answers the 'Why' and 'How' questions for the company.

the 'Why' and the 'How' question you make both the ends and the means intrinsically good. This intrinsic good gives us the best possible leverage to address the prospective employee's motivating need for *Identity* and *Meaning* . The core purpose provides a foundation for *Meaning*, and the core values provide the foundation for creating *Identity*. The Core Ideology should be crafted with this goal in mind. If the company's core ideology matches the employee's view of *Identity* and *Meaning*, then you have an employee you can easily motivate.

If there isn't a perfect fit with the company's core ideology, then you must find a new perfect fit for that individual. The goal is to find opportunities to link the candidate's need for *Identity* and *Meaning* to the work he or she will be engaged in.

This creates a very important role for HR. HR takes the candidate through a process that determines if the individual's passions can fit with the work of the company. Sometimes this is where you find the most powerful motivators.

Fit on this criteria is a Pass/Fail decision. If you don't have someone whose passions link to the work the company does, then you don't have a good fit and you should not hire that person. Let that person find a company where the intrinsic good matches theirs.

How to evaluate the individual's fit.
Make sure every job posting, every job description, and every communication with a potential employee includes the company's Core Ideology. There should be no excuse for the prospective employee not to know the company's Core Ideology.

Begin your interview with the following question: *"Why do you want to work for us?"* You might receive the right answer immediately. *"Because what the company does, it does in order to make the world a better place and I want to be a part of that."* However, it is likely the candidate will be nervous and a little off target in the answer. *"I want to work here because my friend Bob works here and he keeps talking about how terrific it is to work here."* That answer could be followed by, *"What does Bob say is the reason that it's such great place to work?"* And then *"Why does that matter to you?"*.

If this line of questioning does not lead to the information you desire, then you might ask this question, "*What service does the company perform that is important to you personally?*" Hopefully, this will lead the candidate to talk about some intrinsic good in what the company does.

Generally, if you are not getting to genuine passion by this point, it is likely the candidate has not thought this through thoroughly before applying to work in the company. This is probably a point of failure and you should wish the candidate good luck elsewhere.

However, you might sense that the candidate is nervous and you sense there is passion in there somewhere. When people are nervous their ability to think is greatly impaired. You can help this person think it through by asking, "*What is the best job you've ever had?*"[34] Once they've identified that job ask them why that job was the best job. Follow that with, "*Why does this matter?*" And when that is answered, you continue to ask "*Why does that matter?*" And so on until you get to a statement like "*Because it makes the world a better place*", or "*Because it makes people's lives better.*"

Look for passion. If it isn't obvious, don't hire the candidate because that person won't find the work sufficiently motivating. This is a difficult decision, especially when you otherwise love the candidate. However, you don't want to put someone in a job where they are more likely to be miserable than merry; they will tend to drag down others on their team.

College applications often ask applicants to answer the question "*Why do you want to go to school here?*" Administrators complain

---

[34] If this is an entry-level job and the person has no significant experience, ask the person "*Describe the perfect job in terms of what you would like to produce or accomplish*". Then follow the Five Why's described above.

that the answers usually focus on what the student wants to get out of the college experience, the education, and the school itself. Some students will lift themselves above the pack by focusing on their desire to somehow add value to the college. And the rare student has a very specific idea of what they want to do that will enable the college to do something new to benefit humanity in some way.

In the same way, in answering the question, "*Why do you want to work here?*" you would like the candidate to go beyond what they expect to get out of it. You would like them to talk about something bigger. You are looking for passion. You want to hire people who have passion for the 'what' and 'why' of the company. They will be easier to engage, and as a consequence, they will be more productive, more resourceful, better problem-solvers, and generate more profit. They will also tend to be happier and healthier, and they will make it easier to lift the rest of the team.

Behaviors Fit

If you skipped the first chapters of this book, you missed the discussion on values and behavior. Here are the crib notes: Many business experts from Jim Collins to Pat Lencioni, and many others write about the importance of values alignment in guiding behavior. Pat Lencioni

This popular idea ignores 50 years of psychological research which demonstrates that values do not guide behavior. Leadership, accountability, context, and structure all guide behavior. In the final analysis, it is how an employee behaves that determines whether or not they fit with the organization. Some experts talk about values defining the company's culture, however, behavior is what you get. In fact, when asked how to determine what the culture of a company currently is, the answer invariably is "*Look at how people in the company behave.*"

When values and behaviors are not aligned within a company, it is not the values that describe the culture, it's the behaviors. However, this is good news because behaviors are relatively easy to manage as long as you are clear about what behaviors you would like to see.

It is important to be clear here. The values as described earlier are in place to make sure the end and means of the core ideology align. In conjunction with the core purpose they form the basis that allows most employees to find *Identity* and *Meaning* in the work. The core values are not taken as individual items that can be checked off a list; they are part of a whole picture; the core ideology.

We want to avoid making a checklist of values in the hiring decision because people who share values tend to think alike. (Markman 2011) A key competitive goal is to bring in diversity of thought. We want people who see things differently.

When you use values as an integral part of your employee selection process, you are more likely to get people who think alike. Values are tied to how we think about things. In business you want diversity of mind because those different perspectives give you the best ability to see new opportunities and solve problems in creative ways. In the past, the reason many authors pushed for values alignment was because it was commonly believed that values guide behavior. Since values don't do that, you can avoid the trap of hiring like-minded thinkers who share values.

It is behavior that matters.

The good news about behaviors is that when you focus on behaviors there is more room for people with differing values. This diversity of mind leads to different approaches to solving problems. We know that differing values don't prevent people from working well together. Most work places have people who are staunchly conservative sitting side-by-side with people who are staunchly liberal. If they allow these differences to drive their behavior they would most likely be unable to work together.

Remember, before any attempt to find a critical misalignment between a candidate's natural behaviors and the company's desired behaviors, it is essential for the company to establish a behavior grid for the business. Keep in mind that while natural behaviors are easier to work with, almost everyone will behave in the manner defined by the environment.

Once you've identified the behaviors which are critical to the success of the company, choose the five or six most important behaviors. These are generic behaviors that are useful across almost all positions in the company. Use these behaviors to construct 'cases' that you'll ask the candidate to respond to. These case scenarios enable you to see how the candidate will naturally respond to a hypothetical circumstance where the critical behavior should emerge[35].

While we are very open around behavior because it is easy to manage, where you have two candidates that are otherwise equal, this method will become the deciding factor for you.

Here is a case example.

Scenario A
Put yourself in the role of CEO/Owner of the company:

It is two months from the end of the fiscal year. Sales have been strong and all the fixed costs are covered already. Everyone in the company is quite excited because our closed bid has just won

---

[35] As a service we help companies develop these scenarios.

a big University and Hospital water management job from city in a state where the company has never done business before. The city owns and runs the complex. It is a $2.5million deal which means big end-of-year bonuses will be paid to all of the employees.

This morning the head of sales came to you with the following report. Our agent in the distant city has told the head of sales that when we submit the public invoice for the job it should be for $2.8million instead of $2.5million. The company will still get the $2.5million. The extra $300k will be filtered through the agent's offshore shell company and used to pay certain "fees" to local officials in the city council. The agent has assured us that this is completely normal and how things are always done in this city. What do you tell the head of sales to do?

After reading the Scenario above pick 5 words (only 5) out of the 12 below that come to mind as they relate to this situation:

Words	Points
Realistic	-1
Honor	1
Opportunity	-1
Character	1
Revenue	-1
Trustworthy	1
Stature	1
Common Sense	-1
Tolerable	-1
Reputation	1
Real World	-1
Disturbing	1
TOTAL	

Based on Scenario A above, select the course of action you would most likely take:

(1) As distasteful as it is, clearly this is the way things work in that city. Our company will be shielded from legal ramifications because the agent is initiating the payoffs through a safe shell company. This deal is important to all our employees because the end-of-year bonuses will be much larger with this deal and your primary responsibility is to your employees.

(2) You instruct the head of sales to let the agent know that payoffs are unacceptable, unethical, and illegal. We will invoice the original $2.5 million since that is what we bid. If that causes the deal to fall through, then so be it.

(3) You instruct your head of sales to withdraw our offer. We cannot do business with this city as long as the current regime is in power. The reason is simple. Even if we get the deal without paying the extra $300k in pay-offs, everyone who has previously tried to do business with the city will know how things work and will simply assume that we made the required illicit payments.

End of case.

In this case example, the company in question regards its reputation as a key competitive advantage. This is not an easy question to answer, however, the person who naturally values reputation and integrity will pick Option #3. The other two answers are more about a single sale than concern for the long-term reputation of the business.

In discussion this with the candidate, even where they did not choose Option #3 allow them to talk. They should come back around to the realization that the only valid course of action is to walk away from doing business with the regime that currently runs the city.

Scoring

When scoring the 5 words the candidate chooses use the following values and sum the numbers. It is desirable to have a positive score.

Words	Points
Realistic	-1
Honor	1
Opportunity	-1
Character	1
Revenue	-1
Trustworthy	1
Stature	1
Common Sense	-1
Tolerable	-1
Reputation	1
Real World	-1
Disturbing	1
TOTAL	

After you have completed scoring, ask the candidate to elaborate on each of the five words he or she selected. Listen for dialogue that is consistent with a strong sense of reputation. You might ask, *"Tell me why you picked 'xxxxxxxx'?"* Do NOT ask *"Why didn't you pick 'yyyyyyyy'?"* The latter is too much of a leading question.

Even if all the words they choose are negatively scored, they still might say something like, *"I picked the words before giving this full thought. Clearly this is a test of integrity and the company cannot do anything except walk away from this deal."*

Most important in this behavioral section is determining if the candidate is uncomfortable with any of the desired behaviors. While the candidate will conform to the behavioral standard of co-workers, you do not want a candidate whose personal values conflict with the required behaviors. This is a motivational show-stopper. Don't hire that person.

Character Fit

Often companies will include in their values statement what Patrick M. Lencioni calls 'Permission-to-play values'. They represent a given minimum set of values and social behaviors required of any employee in any company.

They include things like: integrity, responsibility, respect, dedication, honesty, teamwork, excellence, accountability, efficiency, accomplishment, persistence, dependability, flexibility, professionalism, ethics, and law-abiding behaviors. These are personal characteristics and they don't distinguish the company from other companies. Nevertheless, make sure the candidate has the personal characteristics the company values most.

We use a toolkit to put structure around this process; you may choose to do this differently. Some companies use a combination of background checks, reference checks and personality tests which may do an adequate job of detecting and measuring the candidate's character. This tends to be less of an issue since good character is far more common than bad character. And, of course, behaviors matter even more than character.

The Bonus Question: The Audition

Even the best screening processes are prone to error. Candidates who do a good job of researching your company will understand your screening methods and attempt to win the offer by gaming each step. One way companies overcome this is to place people in the job on a trial basis and see how they do. At *Method.*, "When we have a few candidates whom we love, we invite them back for our homework assignment, which is, in essence, a live audition." (Ryan, Hiring Method n.d.) If a candidate balks at this process, or pushes back, it's a red card.

Observing a candidate in the actual work environment may be the best way to make the final choice. An independent and anonymous evaluation by the people who interact with the candidates will give you a reasonably balanced picture of their suitability. This provides a quick, simple, and effective mechanism for both determining that the candidate is the right person in the right seat, and for gaining a level of commitment from co-workers because they become invested in this person's future success. This level of personal investment is highly desirable as part of your *Peer-to-Peer Accountability* structure.

Fire the Hiring Manager

At no time in the hiring process do we require the hiring manager to interview the candidate, much less make the final decision on which candidate is the best choice for the position.

That would only invite into the decision a highly biased and poorly trained opinion. It would be foolish to use a hiring process that has been proven less effective. Instead, HR employs a highly professional and disciplined hiring methodology. Keep in mind, you are not only filling a position you are staffing the company.

Self-Motivating Job Structures Tapping into AIMS

One day Ralph Waldo Emerson found himself trying to push a large calf into the barn with his son. The two of them pushed from the rear, pulled from the front, grabbed tail and ears alike. Progress was imperceptible. The best evidence that work was being done were their red faces and perspiration soaked shirts. The calf remained unmoved. Then, along came a servant girl. She grinned and stuck a finger in the calf's mouth. The calf, seduced by this maternal proxy, followed her straight into the barn. Emerson smiled at his son and said, "I like people who know how to get things done!"

We know the best way to get something done is to have self-motivated people working on it. The servant girl tapped into the calf's instinctive motivators. Once the calf was self motivated, he did the necessary work. Likewise, we want to be able to tap into our people's core motivators. This is good on every level. It turns out that a work environment that self-motivates employees not only benefits the company, the bottom-line, and the owners, it also benefits the employees themselves. People who do meaningful work tend to be happier and healthier. At home, happy, healthy breadwinners tend to foster happy and healthy families. These positive outcomes are worthy of the effort necessary to engineer a workplace environment that engenders self-motivation.

As we discussed in the Motivation chapter earlier in the book, we chose the AIMS model over many other models. As the HR professional your responsibility is to tailor the job to fit the candidate such that the two primary motivators are powerfully present. They are *Identity* and *Meaning*.

Identity

Identity is how we want to be seen by the people who know us. It is our reputation, position, rank, influence, standing and character. It is the esteem others have for us. *Identity* is a strong motivator. Our social standing is important to us. Richard Feynman, the famous Nobel Prize winning physicist wrote a book called *What Do You Care What Other People Think.* When he was young his girlfriend (and future first wife) often reminded him of this. Feynman may have been less concerned than the average person about what other people thought; however, at some level Feynman did care. After all, he showed up to accept the Nobel Prize in Physics, which is an honor given by others based on how they feel about the recipient's contribution to physics.

It is safe to assume that most people are in the psycho-normal range and that they care about their *Identity*. They care a lot. It is HR's responsibility to structure the job in such a way that it enables the employee to establish and maintain the desired *Identity*. The aspects of *Identity* we are most able to address are reputation, position/rank, and influence/standing.

It is a good idea to build *Identity* into the job before you fill the position. You only have a certain degree of flexibility in this process. Thus, to the extent that you can do the design work for each position before filling the position, the more likely you will get a candidate whom you can motivate. Here are the things to consider:

Reputation

The simplest way to approach reputation is by working with people in the functional department to identify and rank the competencies which are key to the position. As an example, here is a list of a dozen competencies (there are many others).

Competency
- Communicator
- Connector
- Customer Advocate
- Doer
- Influencer
- Leader
- Negotiator
- Organizer
- Problem Solver
- Researcher
- Teacher
- Team member

Ask the department manager and other employees who will be working with the new hire what good reputation a person could create working in this job. Imagine they all suggested the person in the job would have a reputation as a 'doer'. This will help you decide how to structure the job to foster a reputation as a 'doer'. Some element of that job's measurement should be structured around measuring implementation. You want to hire someone who loves being the 'doer'.

Other reputation areas include things like: being the customer advocate; being the expert; being an empathetic and supportive person (good listener and good person to talk things over with); or being the mediator (the person who can help resolve disputes). Build the job to enable that reputation to blossom. The point is to identify the possible reputations before you look for the right person for the job.

Position/Rank

Nobody wants to be at the bottom of the heap. People prefer to be at the top of a heap. For an organization that is often viewed (incorrectly) as a strict command and control organization, the military does a pretty good job of addressing this issue. Most jobs in the military provide the individual with some sense of superior position. We talked about the Corporal rank earlier. The Corporal is a low rank in the military, however, it is described as a leadership role with command of the most basic unit in the army. The Corporal is part of the Non-Commissioned Officer (NCO) Corps, which is considered the true backbone of the military. It is a position that has its own dignity and esteem and pride.

Every position in the company should be described in this positive way. As we mentioned earlier, if the role were not essential, it would not exist. As it is essential, the company could not function to perfection without it. When describing the duties and responsibilities of the position, highlight the job's essential importance. In doing so, you are building in position and rank, such that each job affords an opportunity to be on 'top of a heap'.

Some organizations achieve this by inverting the organization chart. The person who is usually lowest on the organization chart is now on the top. Since the bulk of these people are often customer-facing employees, the very top of the chart usually has a box for the customer. This is a model of support. Everyone below the customer facing employees on the organization chart are there to support and enable the customer facing employees to do their most-critical job: working with the customer. This perspective makes it easier to describe the roles in positive terms of rank. The truth is, everyone is responsible to someone. A CEO is responsible to the board of directors. The inverted view is that the board of directors are there to help the CEO be successful.

Influence/Standing

A good step in establishing *Identity* is to design the job to allow the employee to establish himself or herself as an authority on something. In senior management roles this is often assumed: the CIO is expected to be the resident expert on information technology systems. However, at lower ranks this critical step is often skipped. Whenever possible, identify the piece of unique knowledge associated with the position. For example: customer service people usually have much better insights into what customers actually think. These insights can be somewhat inconsistent as compared to focus group results. This is a key opportunity to recognize the customer service representative as having something authoritative to say about the customer.

This level of authority should be described with every position. It gives even the lowest rank employee the ability to establish standing in some important area, thereby enabling the employee to feel *Identity* and to create self-motivation.

Meaning

For most people, *Meaning* is perhaps the strongest self-motivator. The things we do create *Meaning* for us. When we perform charitable acts it is not only because they are good for the direct beneficiary, charitable acts also make us feel better about ourselves.

Meaning is deeply personal. Muhammad Yunus, who won the Nobel Peace in 2006 understood the power of work to create self-worth. At one point his Grameen bank established a set of five stars to signify a set of achievements for each branch. When a branch achieved all five goals, the branch received all five stars. No financial incentives were attached to achieving the goals, yet the Grameen staff pursued these stars with a passion. In his book *Banker to the Poor*, Yunus wrote, "They are not doing it for any monetary benefit. They are doing it...to prove their worth to themselves." (Yunus 1999)

Start with the company's core purpose. A well articulated core purpose can provide the foundation upon which individual jobs can be linked to *Meaning*.

Meaning is generally derived from doing something good, or creating something new, or solving something difficult. Different people are excited at different levels by these kinds of outcomes. Finding out what 'turns them on' allows you to build *Meaning* into the job structure.

For example, let's say you have someone who describes themselves as a problem solver. While this is an *Identity* statement it reveals how you might enable them to create *Meaning*. Imagine they work in the plant on the production line. Enable that employee to identify and solve production problems. This will help that employee create the *Meaning* that will drive discretionary effort and thinking. When they do that, a little recognition for the cleverness of their solution goes a long way to enhance the *Meaning* and to help create *Identity*.

This should not be something that is left to chance. HR plays the key role here to structure the job such that it creates *Meaning* for the employee. When the employee is brought on board this will be discussed openly and handed off to the peer group.

Handoff

Once an employee is on board the motivational baton is passed to the peer group for the new employee. HR is responsible to communicate with the group, and show them how this new employee might create *Identity* and *Meaning* in the new job. As we've discussed, a big part of the peer group's job is to ensure that the *Identity* and *Meaning* motivators are working for this employee. This is an ongoing activity.

The leader also plays a key role in enabling the employee to create a sense of *Identity* and *Meaning*. This takes careful thought, careful planning, and forthright execution. If the leader keeps *Identity* and *Meaning* in mind when dealing with the subordinates, then those employees are far more likely to generate higher levels of performance.

The golden rule for leaders is Walk-the-Talk. If the leadership team feels even a tiny bit exempt from the tenets in your behavior grid, then eventually everyone else will too. Business authors often write about the importance of leadership for producing results. This is most true on the negative side. As we pointed out earlier, Wesley Clark and the US Army discovered that it is much easier for leaders to get in the way of success than to enable it. Good leaders enable success. It is the employees themselves who produce it. In some respects the biggest risk for a business owner isn't some lurking black swan; it's the mercurial behavior of management.

The Functional Manager as Leader

That's not to say that great leaders cannot have a great impact. They certainly can. However, the success comes from the ranks.

A few years ago, Grant Halverson took over a $400 million enterprise, which was losing money, he faced a huge problem. The staff had been thoroughly beaten-up by the prior CEO causing morale to be extremely low. Nothing was working internally, and externally they faced a mature marketplace with tough, smart competitors. Worst of all, money was flowing out the back door in the form of losses.

Grant did a number of things to change the environment, and behaviors. Perhaps the most inspired move was what he did with his leadership team. He played musical chairs with them. Each of these department heads got a new assignment. This included the head of sales, IT, operations, risk, finance, and marketing. For example, the head of IT became the head of operations. This invested every team member in the success of his or her colleague. By necessity, they needed to work together. It also meant that the minds at the top of each department were now fresh and open. This allowed lots of ideas to flourish.

What Grant understood was that at every level in the company, a managers primary role is one of leadership. A manager's technical and functional role diminishes as his or her 'people' responsibilities increase. His team produced phenomenal results especially when you keep in mind they were in a mature industry with smart competitors. Half a dozen years into his tenure, with the same staff as he'd inherited, he and his team grew revenues from $400 million to $6.3 billion, market share quadrupled, and the annual return to investors exceeded 30%. (Burnett 2009)

Great managers are leaders. Leaders strive to get the best from the people they are called upon to lead. That is the principal role of a functional manager: to get the best from the people they lead whomever they are.

Despite their opinions of themselves, great leaders have no particular expertise in hiring people.

When Leadership Fails
If you do a good job of hiring people who Grasp It, Desire It, Master It, with the right Behaviors Fit, Passion Fit, and Personal Characteristics, you might still have situations where the newly hired person doesn't thrive. It could be that something was missed in hiring that person. It could also be that the peer group is unable to tap into the motivators for this employee.

The first thing you might do is to find another role for the person in the company and see how he or she works out in the new position. On the flip side, if you have a pattern of this occurring repeatedly with a particular leader or a particular peer group, then HR should take a coaching role and attend the Rated 10 Meetings. People who don't fit with the Behaviors, Passion and Personal Characteristics of the company should be allowed to find success elsewhere.

Behavioral Advantage™ gives the HR executive the opportunity to elevate his or her role in the company. For this to manifest, the HR executive must play a fundamental, ongoing role in ensuring that the business runs smoothly; that the right behaviors emerge; the leadership supports both behaviors and motivators; and that the context, structure, and accountabilities are in place and working effectively, especially *Peer-to-Peer Accountability* . When a behavior seems to be getting out-of-line, the CEO ought to be able to look to the head of HR to take ownership of the problem. Likewise, when the company flourishes, the HR manager has the right to feel proud

Bibliography

Aknin, Lara B, et al. *Prosocial Spending and Well-Being: Cross-Cultural Evidence for a Psychological Universal.* Academic Working Paper, 1 University of British Columbia – Psychology Department, 2 University of British Columbia – Economics Department, 3 Centre for Applied Positive Psychology, 4 Mbarara University of Science and Technology, 5 Makerere University, 6 University of Groningen, 7 Harvard Business School, Harvard Business School, 2010.

AON Hewitt. *2012 Trends in Global Employee Engagement.* Engagement, Chicago: Aon Hewitt, 2012.

Ariely, Dan. *Predictably Irrational: The Hidden Forces That Shape Our Decisions.* New York: HarperCollins Publishers, 2008.

—. *The (Honest) Truth About Dishonesty: How We Lie to Everyone---Especially Ourselves.* New York: HarperCollins Publishers, 2012.

—. *The Upside of Irrationality: The Unexpected Benefits of Defying Logic at Work and at Home.* New York: HarperCollins Publishers, 2010.

Burnett, Bill. *Advantage: Business Competition in the New Normal.* Libertyville, IL: W Burnett LLC, 2009.

Clark, Edie, and Mike Flagg. "Money Isn't Everything to Workers in Small Businesses; A Company's Culture and Their Work Satisfaction Matter More." *National Association of Professional Employer Organizations.* Aug 2007. http://www.napeo.org/media/pressreleases/pr_082907money.

cfm?printPage=1& (accessed Jan 10, 2013).

Clark, Wesley K. *A Time to Lead.* New York: Palgrave MacMillan, 2007.

Collins, James, and Jerry Porras. "Building Your Company's Vision." *Harvard Business Review*, September 1, 1996: 65-77.

Collins, Jim. "Aligning Action and Values." *The Forum.* June 2000. http://www.jimcollins.com/article_topics/articles/aligning-action.htm (accessed Oct 21, 2012).

—. *Good to great: why some companies make the leap...and others don't.* New York, NY: HarperCollins Publishers Inc, 2001.

Diller, Steve, Nathan Shedroff, and Darrel Rhea. *Making Meaning: how Successful Businesses Deliver Meaningful Customer Experiences.* Berkeley , CA: New Riders, 2006.

Frohman, Mark A. "Team Leadership - Three Key Functions Part 3." *Ezine Articles.* http://ezinearticles.com/?Team-Leadership---Three-Key-Functions-Part-3&id=3980132 (accessed 12 22, 2012).

Guthrie, Doug. "Creative Leadership: Trust." *Forbes.com.* June 27, 2012. http://www.forbes.com/sites/dougguthrie/2012/06/27/creativ e-leadership-trust/ (accessed Feb 2, 2013).

Haid, Michael, and Jamie Sims. "Employee Engagement: Maximizing Organizational Performance." *Right Management.* 2009. http://www.right.com/thought-leadership/research/employee-engagement---maximizing-organizational-performance.pdf (accessed May 16, 2013).

Haidt, Jonathan. *The Happiness Hypothesis: Finding Modern Truth in Ancient Wisdom.* Cambridge, MA: Basic Books, 2006.

Harnish, Verne. *Mastering the Rockefeller Habits.* Ashburn, VA: Gazelles Inc., 2002.

Harter, James K, Frank L Schmidt, Emily A Killham, and Sangeeta Agrawal. "The Relationship Between Engagement at Work and Organizational Outcomes." *Gallup.* Aug 2009. http://www.gallup.com/strategicconsulting/126806/Q12-Meta-Analysis.aspx (accessed Oct 22, 2012).

Henrich, Joseph, Steven J Heine, and Ara Norenzayan. "The Weirdest People in the World?" *Behavioral and Brain Sciences,* 2010: 1-75.

Janss, Jeroen, and Jorn Janssens. "The 2012 Global Workforce Study: Engagement at risk, driving strong performance in a volitile global environment." *Towers Watson.* 2012. http://www.towerswatson.com/assets/pdf/7906/GWS-Belgium.pdf (accessed Dec 9, 2012).

Kahle, Lynn, Sharron E. Beatty, and Pamela Homer. "Alternative Measurement Approaches to Consumer Values: The List of Values (LOV) and Life Styles (VALS)." *Journal of Consumer Research 13,* 1986: 405-409.

Kahneman, Daniel. *Thinking Fast and Slow.* New York, NY: Farrar, Straus and Giroux, 2011.

Krafcik, John. "Learning From NUMMI." Unpublished, MIT, Sloan School of Management, 1986.

Kreisman, Barbara J. *Identification of the drivers of employee dissatisfaction and turnover.* Dissertation, University of Texas,

Austin: Unpublished Doctoral Dissertation, 2002.

Lencioni, Patrick M. "Make Your Values Mean Something." *Harvard Business Review* (HBR Press), Jul 2002.

Lencioni, Patrick. *The Advantage: Why Organizational Health Trumps Everything Else In Business.* San Francisco, CA: Jossey-Bass, 2012.

Lovallo, Dan, Olivier Sibony, and Daniel Kahneman. "The Big Idea: Before You Make That Big Decision..." *Harvard Business Review* (HBR Press), June 2011.

LRN Corporation. "HOW Metrics." *LRN Inspiring Principled Performance.* 7 1, 2011. http://www.lrn.com/howmetrics/ (accessed 12 30, 2012).

Lundin, Stephen C, Harry Paul, and John Christensen. *Fish! A Remarkable Way to Boost Morale and Improve Results.* New York, NY: Hyperion, 2000.

Markman, Art. "Why Do We Like People Who Like the Music We Do?" *Psychology Today.* Aug 9, 2011. http://www.psychologytoday.com/blog/ulterior-motives/201108/why-do-we-people-who-the-music-we-do (accessed 12 12, 2012).

Milgram, Stanley. "Behavioral Study of Obedience." *Journal of Abnormal and Social Psychology 67*, April 1963: 371-8.

—. *Obedience to Authority; an Experimental View.* New York: Harper & Row, 1974.

Moss, Sherry. "Finding Meaning in Working at Walmart." *Huffpost Healthy Living.* The Huffington Post.

http://www.huffingtonpost.com/sherry-moss/finding-meaning-work_b_822876.html (accessed 12 22, 2012).

Norton, M.I., L Anik, E.W. Dunn, and J Quoidbach. "Prosocial Incentives Increase Employee Satisfaction and Team Performance." Paper Presented, Canadian Psychological Association, Halifax, 2012.

Pierce, Lamar, and Jason Snyder. "Ethical Spillovers in Firms: Evidence from Vehicle Emissions Testing." *Management Science*, November 1, 2008.

Porath, Christine, and Christine Pearson. "The Price of Incivility: Lack of Respect Hurts Morale--and the Bottom Line." *Harvard Business Review* (HBR Press), Jan-Feb 2013: 114-121.

Ritter, AL. *The 100/0 Principle: The Secret of Great Relationships.* Naperville, IL: Simple Truths, 2010.

Rodgers, Robert, and John E Hunter. "Impact of management by objectives on organizational productivity." *Journal of Applied Psychology* 76, no. 2 (April 1991): 322-336.

Rokeach, Milton. *The Nature of Human Values.* New York: Free Press, 1973.

Ryan, Eric. "Looking For Talent? Here Are Three Steps To Making The Right Hire." *Fast Company Co.Design.* http://www.fastcodesign.com/1664026/looking-for-talent-here-are-three-steps-to-making-the-right-hire.

Ryan, Eric, and Adam Lowry. *The Method Method: Seven Obsessions That Helped Our Scrappy Start-up Turn an Industry Upside-down.* New York: Portfolio Penguin, 2011.

Salam, Abdus. *Unification of fundamental forces.* New York, NY: Cambridge University Press, 1990.

Sanborn, Pete, Rahul Malhotra, and Amy Atchison. "Trends in Global Employee Engagement." *Aon Hewitt.* 2011. http://www.aon.com/attachments/thought-leadership/Trends_Global_Employee_Engagement_Final.pdf (accessed Dec 9, 2012).

Sartain, Libby, and Martha I Finney. *HR from the Heart: Inspiring stories and strategies for building the people side of great business.* New York, NY: AMACOM, American Management Association, 2003.

Seaman, John T., and George David Smith. "Your Company's History as a Leadership Tool: Take your organization forward by drawing on the past." *Harvard Business Review*, December 1, 2012.

Sherif, Muzafer. "A study of some social factors in perception: Chapter 3." *Archives of Psychology* 27, no. 187 (1935): 23-46.

Sherif, Muzafer. "An experimental approach to the study of attitudes." *Sociometry* 1 (1937): 90-98.

Showkeir, Jamie, and Maren Showkeir. *Authentic Conversations: Moving from Manipulation to Truth and Commitment.* San Francisco, CA: Berrett-Koehler Publishers, Inc, 2008.

Stanford University Graduate School of Business. "Case HR-11, New United Motors Manufacturing, Inc." November 19, 2004. https://gsbapps.stanford.edu/cases/documents/HR11.pdf (accessed May 16, 2013).

Sutton, Robert I. *Good boss, bad boss: how to be the best...and learn from the worst.* New York, NY: Business Plus, Hachette Book Group, 2010.

Sutton, Robert I. *Weird Ideas That Work: How to build a Creative Company.* New York: Free Press, 2002.

Thompson, Alex. "Interpreting Kahle's List of Values: Being Respected, Security, and Self-Fulfillment in Context." *UW-L Journal of Undergraduate Research XII (2009)*, 2009: 1-9.

Toyota. "Toyoda Precepts: The base of the Global Vision." *Toyota.* Toyota. April 2012. http://www.toyota-global.com/company/toyota_traditions/company/apr_2012.html (accessed Oct 23, 2012).

University of Foreign Military and Cultural Studies. *Red Team Handbook.* Vol. 6.0. Washington DC: US Government, 2012.

Van Allen, Sarah. "The Next Discipline Applying Behavioral Economics to Drive Growth and Profitability." *Gallup.* 2009. http://www.gallup.com/strategicconsulting/122906/next-discipline.aspx (accessed Oct 22, 2012).

Whiteley, Paul. *Are Britons Becoming More Dishonest.* Academic, University of Essex, Essex: University of Essex, 2012.

Wickman, Gino. *Traction: Get a grip on your business.* Livonia, MI: EOS, 2007.

Yunus, Muhammad. *Banker to the Poor.* New York, NY: PublicAffairs, 1999.

Index

About THNK

THNK (pronounced "think") has pulled together over 150 years of leadership experience, along with the most enlightening psychological studies on behavior, to develop a structured methodology that is easy to implement and sustainable. Demanding the right business behaviors while simultaneously eliminating behaviors that undermine performance delivers exceptional results.

Company Leadership

Bill Burnett, Co-Founder

Raj Jayaraman, Co-Founder

Anup Manchanda, Co-Founder

Howard B. Schwedel, Co-Founder

Glenn M. Turner, Co-Founder

Dedication

Bill Burnett dedicates this book:

- To my wife Linda who has generously supported my efforts to get this book to its current condition.
- To my children, George, Madeleine, and Charlie who continue to be a source of great joy to me.

Anup Manchanda dedicates this book:

- To my parents Manohar and Prabha, who have always walked the talk and set an example for me to follow.
- To my kids Neha and Anokhi to look inside themselves and always exhibit a desired behavior.
- To Rachel who brings *Meaning* and *Identity* to my life.
- To my colleagues – Bill, Glenn, Howard and Raj for inspiring me to deliver results that are above and beyond.

Raj Jayaraman dedicates this book:

- To my aunt Uma who has been fighting breast cancer for the last 4 years. Her tenacity, courage, positive attitude and determination gives me the strength to fight and never give up on any obstacles or challenges.
- To my wife Vishali and kids Kashyap and Shreya who bring joy to my life.

- Cont.

Howard Schwedel dedicates this book:

- To those that love and support me, no matter what!
  - Sandy my beautiful wife and better half by far.
  - Jeff and Melissa who continually make me proud to be their Dad.
- And a shout out to the Co-Founders of THNK.
  - Anup who formed the group that became THNK.
  - Bill who I continue to learn from and who insists we have fun in the process.
  - Glenn who demonstrates the qualities that others trust and depend upon.
  - Raj for the energy level he brings to THNK.

Glenn Turner dedicates this book:

- To my Dad who has been an inspirational leader for my entire family through good times and bad
- To My Daughters Amber, Shannon and Tristen who are the light of my life
- To Body my first Grandchild who is a joy and pleasure to be around.

25189497R00121

Made in the USA
Lexington, KY
15 August 2013